THE DEMAND
FOR MONEY

THE DEMAND FOR MONEY
Theories and Evidence

SECOND EDITION

David E.W. Laidler

The University of Western Ontario

DUN-DONNELLEY—A Dun & Bradstreet Company

New York

Library of Congress Cataloging in Publication Data

Laidler, David E. W.
  The demand for money.

  Bibliography: p.
  Includes index.
  1. Money. 2. Money—Mathematical models. I. Title.
HG221.L24   1977   332.4'01   77-2133
ISBN 0-912212-07-1

Dun-Donnelley Publishing Corporation
666 Fifth Avenue
New York, New York 10019

Typography by Christopher Simon

Manufactured in the United States of America

Contents

Preface

The aim of this new edition of *The Demand for Money* is the same as that of the first one. It seeks to give an up-to-date account of what is known about this particular branch of macroeconomics in a fashion that will make it accessible to undergraduate economics majors and beginning graduate students. Since the first edition was written in 1967–1968, three developments have taken place that are particularly relevant to its subject matter.

First, the *IS-LM* framework has lost its position as the centerpiece of short-run macroeconomics. Even so, I have chosen to begin again with an account of this model largely unchanged from the first edition. Although it no longer dominates short-run macroeconomics, the *IS-LM* model is still an important element of the subject. A great deal of the work done on the demand for money, with which this book deals, investigated questions raised by the model; and to understand that work fully, the reader must first of all be familiar with it. Moreover, it is an important aspect of any student's education to learn that economics is an evolving body of knowledge and not an unchanging package of well understood principles and facts. Much work originally conceived of against the background of the *IS-LM* model has in fact ended up contributing to the undermining of its central position in macroeconomics. By starting with an account of this model, I hope in this new edition to be able to show the reader something of the way in which theoretical and empirical work have interacted over the last decade to change our perception of the way in which the macroeconomy functions.

Second, much theoretical work has been done in the last 10 years on behavior implied by the precautionary motive for holding money. By and large, this work is very technical and beyond the reach of the average undergraduate, but it nevertheless contains ideas to which students ought to be exposed. To deal with this problem, I have devised my own extremely simple, precautionary demand model and included an account of it in the otherwise largely unchanged section of the book dealing with theories of the demand for money (Part II). I hope readers will find that it captures the basic points made by recent contributors to the field without doing too much harm to the technical sophistication which has characterized their work.

Finally, a great deal of empirical evidence on the demand for money has been amassed in the last 10 years, and the final part of this book has been almost completely rewritten to reflect this. In 1968, it was possible to attempt, in those chapters, a fairly comprehensive survey of the then existing empirical literature. In 1977 the literature has grown to such an extent that, although I hope my coverage of the relevant issues is comprehensive, the list of articles to which I refer is somewhat selective. Compared to the first edition I have paid more attention to work done on economies other than that of the United States and, closely related, devoted more time to evidence concerning the role of the inflation rate in the demand-for-money function. Above all, much more emphasis is now placed on work concerned with investigating the lag structure of the demand-for-money function. Such work was in its infancy when the first edition of this book was written but now forms an important body of literature in its own right whose results and implications have extended, and to a degree changed, our understanding of monetary economics.

As with the first edition, I have tried to keep the level of exposition such that a student who has completed an intermediate macroeconomics course will be able to follow the bulk of the arguments presented. However, because of the introduction of a section on the precautionary demand for money, Chapter 5 will be easier to read for the student who has studied, or is studying, elementary statistics, than for others. This chapter is probably a little more technically demanding than the others, because elsewhere it has proven possible to confine specifically mathematical material to appendices. Even so, I do not think that the arguments presented there will prove to be beyond the grasp of the average undergraduate, if he or she is willing to make some extra effort to master them.

Joel Fried, Jacob Frenkel, Peter Howitt, Benjamin Klein, and Richard Towey, read the manuscript of this edition at various stages, and made helpful comments. Alastair Murdoch, Hasan Imam, and Michael Veall, graduate students at the University of Western Ontario, drew my attention to a particularly silly mistake in Chapter 5. Sad to say, any other mistakes, silly or otherwise, must remain my sole responsibility.

Introduction

The basic problems dealt with by macroeconomics are the determination of the level of national income and employment, the determination of the price level and its rate of change, and the determination of the long-run rate of growth of income. In order to deal with these problems economists have found it necessary to construct models of the macroeconomy that take into account many more variables than those they are primarily interested in understanding.

Although there exists a substantial literature on the role of monetary factors in economic growth models, it is nevertheless the case that money has never played as central a role in the analysis of growth processes as it has in that of short-run price and income determination.

The predictions that short-run models make about the interrelationships between variables in the economy depend critically upon what is assumed to be true about the manner in which the supply and demand for money interact. It is not possible to deduce from any first principles which particular assumptions about the money market are the most reasonable. Strong a priori cases can be made out in support of several differing theories of how the money market operates. It is only by reference to empirical evidence that any conclusion about which theory is the most acceptable can be reached.

It is the primary aim of this book to describe the current state of knowledge about the demand side of the money market. The first two chapters set out the macroeconomic model that forms the core of most textbooks on the subject and show how the money market fits into it. It is also shown how different views about the nature of the demand-for-money function lead to different and sometimes contradictory conclusions about how the model works as a whole. Part II turns to a more detailed discussion of the theories underlying the various forms of the demand-for-money function that can be included in such a macroeconomic model. Part III describes and assesses these competing theories in the light of available empirical evidence and offers some suggestions about the broader macroeconomic implications of this evidence.

PART

I

THE DEMAND FOR MONEY IN A MACROECONOMIC FRAMEWORK

1

A Simple Macroeconomic Model

Short-run macroeconomics deals largely with the determination of the level of national income, the level of employment, and the price level. In particular, it tries to single out the factors that might be expected to lead to fluctuations in these variables. It also tries to analyze how those variables under the control of the government can be used to offset such fluctuations when they are undesirable and to bring them about when they are desirable. In order to deal with such questions it is helpful to have an explicit model of the economy, and the one we describe here was, for virtually 2 decades, almost universally accepted as the core of short-run macroeconomics. Though there were debates and disagreements enough about macroeconomic matters, they were carried on against a background of the common frame of reference provided by this model. The model in question no longer occupies quite so central a position in macroeconomics, though it is still one of its vital elements.

It has lost its dominant position for two reasons. First, as we shall see, it is a model that helps us analyze the determinants of real income and employment given the constancy of the price level, or the determinants of the price level given the level of income and employment. It does not enable us to deal with questions concerning the interaction of price level and output fluctuations, and such questions are central to the analysis of the "stagflation" phenomenon which has been the dominant macroeconomic policy problem of the last decade. Other models have had to be developed to confront these important issues. Second, the very research this framework prompted in the first place generated results that began to undermine it.

This book deals with the results produced by one important segment of that research. If the reader is fully to appreciate the results presented here, he must see them in the context of the theoretical framework in terms of which they were generated. For this reason alone the model set out in this and the next chapter is worth his attention. Only when this model has been mastered will he be in a position to understand the significance of work on the demand for money for macroeconomics. The ways in which the results of this work require the basic macroeconomic framework to be modified and extended are the subject of the last chapter of this book.

The Model

Let us now turn to the basic macroeconomic model. It is customary to deal with its behavior in unemployment situations first, and we follow this procedure here.

Let us assume that the economy to be analyzed is one in which there are available enough productive resources to supply the goods needed to meet any level of aggregate demand that may arise. Let us also assume that changes in the level of aggregate demand for goods and services are met solely by output changes, and that the price level can be taken as given at some historically determined level.†

---

† It is implicitly assumed here that capital and labor enter production in fixed proportions so that there is no tendency for the marginal product of labor to fall as employment increases, since the employment of capital increases along with that of labor. The combination of this assumption with that of a fixed level of money wages produces a level of prices that is independent of the level of output. A more complex model, which allows capital and labor to be used in variable proportions and also assumes full employment of capital, generates a positive functional relationship between the price level and output for a given wage level. There is no important qualitative difference between these models as far as matters at hand are concerned, so we have chosen to deal with the simpler one. The reader will find the more complicated model fully described in Smith (1956).

In this economy, expenditure can be made by households, in which case it is called *consumption*, by firms, in which case it is called *investment*, or by the government, in which case it is called *government expenditure*. The usual assumptions are made about the determinants of these components of expenditure. Consumption is thought of as being an increasing function of disposable income and, since it is for the moment convenient to deal with an economy in which there are no taxes, this means that consumption can be treated simply as a function of income. It is also postulated that the marginal propensity to consume is less than one. Investment is thought of as being negatively related to the rate of interest, while government expenditure is treated as exogenous—that is, as a variable that may affect but is not affected by the other variables in the model. The model is in equilibrium when the level of expenditure in the economy, as determined by these functions, is equal to the level of income, and in Figure 1-1 the reader will find the model set out in familiar geometric terms. (*Note:* In labeling the figures in this book, subscripts in parentheses have

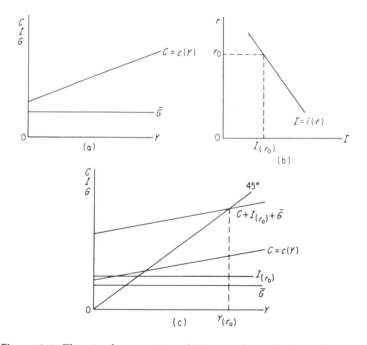

Figure 1-1. The simple geometry of income determination. C is consumption, I is investment, G is government expenditure, Y is income, and r is the rate of interest. c and i denote functional relationships, while the bar over G indicates that it is an exogenous variable.

been attached to many variables. This notation indicates that the variable carrying the subscript takes the value it does given that the variable in the subscript takes the value mentioned in the subscript. For example, in Figure 1-1, $Y_{(r_0)}$ indicates the value income takes given that the rate of interest takes the value r_0. Panel (a) shows the consumption function $C = c(Y)$ and the exogenous level of government expenditure $\bar{G}$, while the investment function $I = i(r)$ is plotted in panel (b). If it is assumed that the rate of interest is fixed at level r_0, the level of investment will be determined at $I_{(r_0)}$. In panel (c) this level of investment is added to consumption and government expenditure to produce the curve $C + I_{(r_0)} + \bar{G}$ which gives the relationship implicit in the model between the level of aggregate expenditure and the level of income. The 45° line plots all the points at which aggregate expenditure, measured on the vertical axis, can be equal to income, measured on the horizontal axis. That is, it is a geometric representation of the equilibrium condition of the model. The aggregate expenditure curve crosses this line at the only point at which expenditure as determined by the functional relationships involved in the model is equal to the level of income.

$Y_{(r_0)}$ is then the equilibrium level of income, but only so long as the rate of interest remains at r_0. If it takes some other value, so will the level of investment, and the equilibrium level of income will be different. Implicit in the relationship discussed up to now is a relationship between the value of the rate of interest and the equilibrium level of income, and it is easy enough to make this relationship explicit.

Figure 1-2(a) shows the relationship between investment and the rate of interest. Panel (b) shows various relationships between aggregate expenditure and income, each based on the same consumption function and level of government expenditure, but each assuming that the rate of interest takes a different value: r_1 is a lower interest rate than r_0, while r_2 is lower still. The lower the rate of interest the higher the level of investment, as Figure 1-2(a) tells us, and the higher the level of investment the higher the level of aggregate expenditure. Thus, in Figure 1-2(b), $C + I_{(r_2)} + \bar{G}$ lies above $C + I_{(r_1)} + \bar{G}$, which in turn lies above $C + I_{(r_0)} + \bar{G}$. Corresponding to each of these aggregate expenditure curves is an equilibrium level of income. As can readily be seen, the lower the level of the rate of interest the higher this level of income. This relationship between the rate of interest and the equilibrium level of income is plotted as the curve IS in Figure 1-2(c). (IS refers to the fact that in a model without government expenditure any point along this curve is one at which investment is equal to saving.

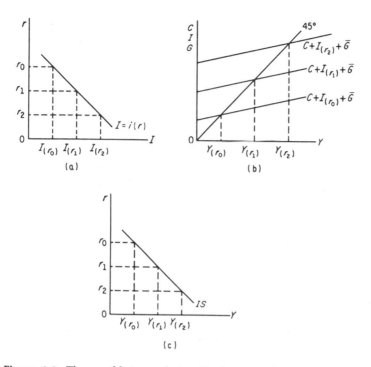

Figure 1-2. The equilibrium relationship between the rate of interest and the level of income implicit in the model of the real-goods market.

It is now general to use this label for any curve showing real-goods market equilibrium.)

The foregoing analysis at first sight presents us with a problem, for, as Figure 1-2(c) shows quite explicitly, the model with which we are dealing can tell us what the equilibrium level of income is if we know the rate of interest, or, for that matter, what the rate of interest is if we know the equilibrium level of income. It would be useful to have a model that could tell us what the equilibrium level of income is without first having to know what the rate of interest is, but this model is not up to the task. It is incomplete, which should not be too surprising. After all, not only do people make decisions about current flows of goods and services, about how much to consume, about how much to invest, and so on, they also make decisions about stocks, about how to hold what may loosely be called their wealth. These two sets of decisions are not independent of one another, and a model that deals with only one of them may be expected to turn out incomplete. As we shall now see, the macroeconomic model with which we are dealing here may be completed by paying some attention to the problems involved in wealth holding and by looking at the way in which such problems interact with those involved in decisions about flows of goods and services.

There are many ways of holding wealth. An individual can own consumer durable goods, corporate equities, bonds, and so forth, but for purposes of extending our simple macroeconomic model it is sufficient to assume that there are only two types of assets available—money and bonds. The problem facing individuals as far as holding their wealth is concerned is how to allocate it between money and bonds. If we take the level of wealth as given, if money is not held bonds must be, and the problem reduces to how much money to hold. The rest of this book is devoted to examining various hypotheses as to what variables are involved in this decision, but for the moment we merely assert a commonly held simple hypothesis about the determinants of the demand for money and see how it can be fitted into our model. It is usually argued that at a given price level the demand for money depends primarily on the level of income and the rate of interest, and that, if the price level varies while other variables remain unchanged, the demand for money will vary in exact proportion to the price level. This is equivalent to asserting that the demand for money measured in units of constant purchasing power, that is, in real terms, does not vary with the price level.

Because money is a universally acceptable means of exchange, it is argued that the demand for it increases with income. It is also pointed out that, since bond holding is the alternative to money holding, interest income is forgone by holding money. The higher is the rate of interest the higher is the opportunity cost of holding money, so, it is argued, the lower is the demand for money. As to the supply side of the money market, it is usual to assume as a first approximation that the supply of money is completely under the control of monetary authorities whose behavior may be treated as exogenous to the model. As with any supply-and-demand problem, this market is in equilibrium when the supply and demand for money are equal.

Figure 1-3 deals with the market in geometric terms. In panel (a) is graphed the demand for money as it is related to the rate of interest at the level of income Y_0. With a given money supply and price level, this market will be in equilibrium when the rate of interest is equal to $r_{(Y_0)}$. As far as the money market is concerned, however, we have a

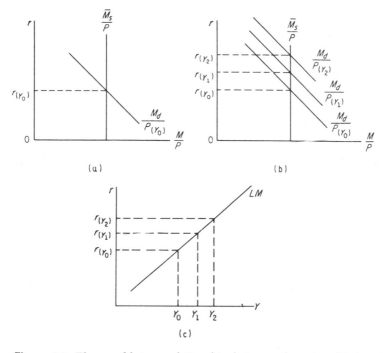

Figure 1-3. The equilibrium relationship between the rate of interest and the level of income implicit in the model of the money market. M is the quantity of money, and P is the price level, so that M/P is the quantity of money measured in units of constant purchasing power. The subscripts s and d stand for supplied and demanded, and the bar over M_s indicates that it is an exogenous variable.

problem analogous to the one we met earlier in the context of the market for current flows of goods and services. The equilibrium value the market determines for the rate of interest is an equilibrium value only so long as the level of income is at Y_0. Figure 1-3(b) shows this problem clearly enough. Y_2 is a higher level of income than Y_1, which in turn is higher than Y_0. Since the demand for money at any rate of interest increases when the level of income rises, this means that the whole curve relating the demand for money to the rate of interest shifts to the right at higher income levels. With a given money supply and price level, this involves a higher equilibrium interest rate. As far as equilibrium in the money market is concerned, there is implicit in the model a positive relationship between the level of income and the rate of interest. This relationship is plotted in Figure 1-3(c) and is labeled, as is customary, *LM*. (*LM* refers to the fact that, at any point on this curve, the "liquidity preference" is just satisfied by the supply of money.)

We now have two different equilibrium relationships between the rate of interest and the level of income. However, the market for real goods and services is not totally independent of the money market. The people whose decisions underlie the consumption and investment functions are the same people whose behavior vis-a-vis wealth holding determines the demand-for-money function. The level of income and rate of interest involved in both markets are the same, so that the economy as a whole can be in equilibrium only when their values are compatible with equilibrium in both markets. This implies that the values in question must lie on both the *LM* curve and the *IS* curve, and obviously this can occur only where the two curves intersect. In Figure 1-4 the two curves are plotted against the same axes, and the equilibrium level of income is given at Y_e with the rate of interest having an equilibrium value of r_e. These in turn imply equilibrium values for consumption, investment, and money holding, as should be apparent.

Shifts of the IS and LM Curves

Figure 1-4 looks simple enough, consisting as it does of only two intersecting curves, but this simplicity is misleading. Underlying the *IS* curve is a given consumption function and a given investment function, as well as a given level of government expenditure and taxes

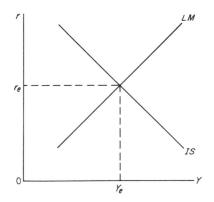

Figure 1-4. The determination in the complete model of the equilibrium levels of the interest rate and of income.

(assumed so far to be equal to zero). Behind the *LM* curve there lies a given demand-for-money function, a given money supply, and a given price level. We must now look at the way the model responds to changes in these underlying factors.

A change in any of the factors underlying the *IS* curve will cause it to shift, and a change in any of the factors underlying the *LM* curve will cause it to shift also. Figure 1-5 shows what the consequences of

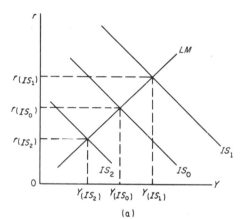

(a)

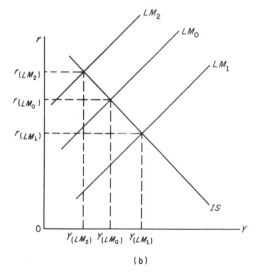

(b)

Figure 1-5. The effect on the equilibrium level of income and the rate of interest of shifting the *IS* curve and the *LM* curve.

such shifts will be. Panel (a) deals with the consequences of shifts of the IS curve and, as will be seen readily enough, should the curve shift upward and to the right from IS_0 to IS_1, the equilibrium level of income and the equilibrium level of the rate of interest will both increase. Should the curve shift to the left from IS_0 to IS_2, the effect will be precisely opposite. If the LM curve shifts to the right from LM_0 to LM_1, the level of income will rise while the rate of interest will fall, as can be seen by inspecting Figure 1-5(b). A shift in this curve to the left, from LM_0 to LM_2, will have precisely the opposite effect.

If these are the effects of shifts of the IS and LM curves, what are the causes? Let us consider the IS curve first; a glance back at Figure 1-2 will be helpful at this stage, since it is there that the derivation of this curve is shown. It will be recalled that the relationship in question between the rate of interest and the level of income is generated because investment is a component of aggregate expenditure, and because it increases as the rate of interest falls. Every point on the IS curve involves a given rate of interest generating a certain level of aggregate expenditure. If the IS curve is to shift, it means that this relationship between the level of aggregate expenditure and the rate of interest must shift. Three factors can be the cause. If, as in Figure 1-6(a), the relationship between the rate of interest and the level of investment shifts to the right, this implies a higher level of aggregate expenditure at any level of the rate of interest [Figure 1-6(b)] so that the IS curve shifts to the right as shown in Figure 1-6(c). A similar argument obviously follows in reverse. If the level of government expenditure increases, again the level of aggregate expenditure increases for any given level of the rate of interest, so that the IS curve again shifts to the right. A cut in government expenditure, as in Figure 1-7(a), has the opposite effect, as should again be obvious. Figure 1-7(b) shows this.

The effect of a shift in the relationship between consumption and income needs looking at with a little care, since it is by shifting the consumption function that taxes have their effect on the economy. Recall that consumption depends upon disposable income and consider Figure 1-8(a) in which taxes are initially assumed to be zero so that the consumption function is first given by $C = c(Y)$. If a tax of a fixed amount T is now levied, the level of income Y_0 will correspond to a disposable income of $Y_0 - T$ and consumption will be equal to $c(Y_0 - T)$. A similar argument holds for any level of income. In the presence of a tax, the consumption function must be shifted to the right to $C = c(Y - T)$ by the amount of the tax in order that it will still

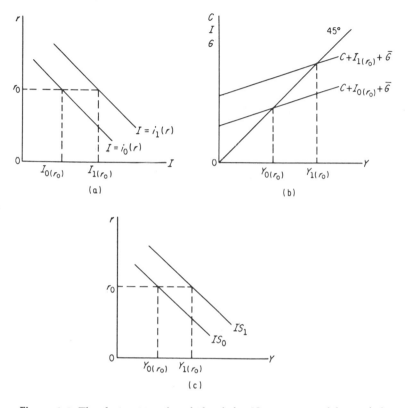

Figure 1-6. The derivation of a shift of the *IS* curve caused by a shift of the investment function.

enable us to determine the level of consumption given the level of before-tax income. This is equivalent to shifting the consumption function downward by an amount equal to the marginal propensity to consume times the amount of the tax, as should be clear from an inspection of Figure 1-8.†

In general, an increase in taxes shifts the consumption function downward and a cut in taxes shifts it up—shifting the aggregate expenditure curve in the same direction and by the same amount. Thus an increase in taxes shifts the *IS* curve to the left, while a cut in taxes

---

† The reader who wishes to make sure that he understands what is going on should try to prove that an equal increase in government expenditure and taxes will shift the *IS* curve to the right by the amount of the increase in government expenditure, that is, that the balanced budget multiplier is equal to one.

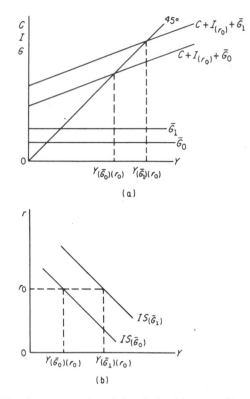

Figure 1-7. The derivation of a shift of the IS curve (b) caused by a change in the level of government expenditure (a). $G_1 > \bar{G}_0$.

shifts it to the right. Although we have here discussed cuts in the *amount* of taxes, the same conclusions follow as far as an alteration in tax *rates* is concerned. A change in a tax rate can always be converted into a change in the amount of taxes paid by multiplying the change in the rate by the level of income. The only change here is that the shift in the consumption function is no longer a parallel one. This is shown in Figure 1-8(b).

Anything that can shift the aggregate expenditure curve upward shifts the IS curve to the right, with the consequences for the level of income and the rate of interest shown in Figure 1-5(a). Let us now see what can cause shifts in the LM curve. As the reader may guess, since the LM curve is derived from a given demand-for-money function with a given supply of money and a given price level, a change in any

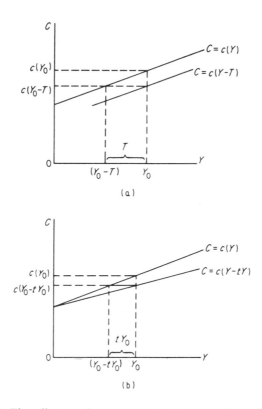

Figure 1-8. The effect on the consumption function of introducing (a) a fixed level of taxation T and (b) proportional taxation at the rate t. Note that a change in taxes is equal to an opposite change in disposable income, so that its effect on consumption at a given level of national income is to reduce it by the marginal propensity to consume times the change in taxes.

of these factors can cause it to shift. Consider changes in the supply of money first. Figure 1-9(a) is similar to Figure 1-3(b), and it can readily be seen that a change in the money supply from $\overline{M}_{s_0}$ to $\overline{M}_{s_1}$ will involve equilibria in the money market that require a lower interest rate for any given level of income. This is reflected in Figure 1-9(b) in a shift of the LM curve from LM_0 to LM_1. By the same reasoning, it can be shown that a cut in the money supply will shift the LM curve to the left.

It is convenient to leave the question of the demand-for-money function and its relationship to the behavior of the model until the

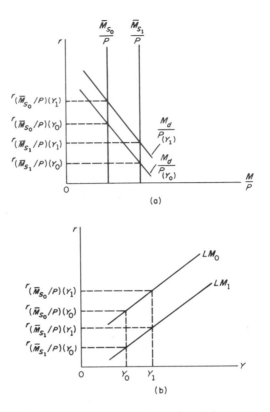

Figure 1-9. The derivation of a shift of the *LM* curve caused by an increase in the money supply.

next chapter, but we still have the matter of the price level. It should be clear that, given the money supply, a fall in the price level will shift the *LM* curve to the right because this has the same effect on the stock of money measured in real terms as increasing the nominal supply of money at a given price level. It should be equally clear that the mechanism will work exactly in reverse in the case of an increase in the price level. This factor will become important when we deal with the model in a full-employment context, as we shall now see.

The Model at Full Employment

So far we have restricted our analysis to unemployment situations and have assumed that, over the time period for which it is relevant, prices can be treated as constant. It is possible to extend this model's

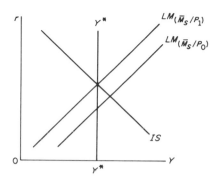

Figure 1-10. The effect on the *LM* curve of a price rise brought about by an initial situation of excess demand. Y^* is the highest level of income that can be attained. $P_1 > P_0$.

field of application by reversing these two assumptions, by allowing prices to become flexible at least in an upward direction while assuming that the level of output is fixed at a level at which all resources in the economy are fully employed. The price level is then thought of as responding to the presence of excess demand. When the combined demands for goods and services of firms, households, and the government exceed what the economy is capable of producing, the price level rises; as we shall see, it is precisely the effect of rising prices on the money market that rids the economy of excess demand and restores the model to equilibrium.

In terms of the analytic framework in which we are working, a situation of excess demand arises when the *LM* and *IS* curves intersect at a level of income higher than the maximum that can be produced.† This level of income is given as Y^* in Figure 1-10. In a situation of excess demand the price level is bid up from its initial value of P_0, and as this happens the supply of money measured in real terms falls and the *LM* curve begins to shift to the left. So long as

---

† It should be clear to the reader that there is an element of approximation involved in postulating a precise level of income that can be identified with full employment. It makes more empirical sense to think of full employment as being a region rather than a point on the income scale. However, to make such a sharp distinction here helps to keep the analysis simple without also making it seriously misleading. The reader should note that aggregate demand is not given by the intersection of the *LM* and *IS* curves when this is at a higher level of income than is attainable. This intersection only shows what aggregate demand would be were this income level attainable.

excess demand persists, this process continues. It ceases when the price level has risen sufficiently to make the quantity of money measured in real terms compatible with the demand for it at Y^* and at the level of the interest rate that conditions in the real-goods market require for equilibrium at Y^*. This occurs when the LM curve has shifted far enough to intersect the IS curve at Y^*. At this point the model is back in equilibrium with a price level of P_1, as shown in Figure 1-10.

This extension of the model to full-employment situations enables us to say a little more than previously about the effects of various changes on the economy. Everything said earlier holds true so long as we deal with falls in aggregate demand. However, if we start out from a situation of full-employment equilibrium, it will be clear that the predictions we have made about the effects of anything that shifts either the IS curve or the LM curve to the right cannot be carried over. These predictions involve increases in the level of income that cannot be brought about. In Figure 1-11(a) the shift of the IS curve so that it intersects the LM curve to the right of Y^* sets in motion a price rise from P_0 which causes the LM curve to shift to the left. The consequence of the shift is ultimately a higher price level P_1 and a higher rate of interest, rather than a higher level of income and a higher rate of interest as in the unemployment case. Similarly, the shift of the LM curve to the right displayed in Figure 1-11(b), caused by an increase in the money supply from M_{s_0} to M_{s_1} creates an excess demand for goods, which results in the price level rising from P_0 until at P_1 the money supply measured in real terms is again compatible with equilibrium—that is, takes the same value it did initially. In this case the price level must move in proportion to the money supply, while the rate of interest remains unchanged.†

---

† These results are generated in terms of a model in which the IS curve is invariant with respect to the price level. At least three complications could be introduced that would alter this. First, in an open economy, the price level may be a variable that is of importance in determining the level of exports, which in turn is a component of aggregate demand. If a higher price level caused lower exports, the IS curve would shift to the left as the price level rose. The price level would then have to rise less than in proportion to any increase in the money supply before the model came back into equilibrium. A progressive tax levied on nominal rather than real income would produce a similar result, since the higher the price level the greater the proportion of real income paid in taxes. The third factor, which works in the same direction, deals with the possible role of wealth in the determination of consumption and is generally known as the *wealth effect*. It is both too subtle and too important in the history of macroeconomics to be

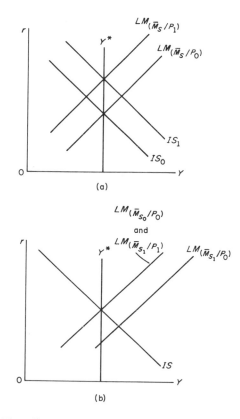

Figure 1-11. The effect of excess demand brought about by (a) a shift of the IS curve and (b) a shift of the LM curve. $M_{s_1} > M_{s_0}$; $P_1 > P_0$; $M_{s_0}/P_1 = M_{s_0}/P_0$.

Summary and Conclusions

We now summarize the results generated in this chapter. It has been shown that, as far as an underemployed economy is concerned, changes in the equilibrium level of income may occur as a result of fluctuations of the investment function and also that they can be

---

dealt with in a footnote. The interested reader may find it treated in Appendix B and should note that the fact that it is dealt with in a brief appendix and not given a chapter reflects not its lack of importance as far as macroeconomics is concerned, but only the fact that it is not concerned with the demand-for-money function per se.

induced by changes in government expenditure and changes in tax rates; increases in government expenditure give rise to increases in the equilibrium level of income, as do cuts in taxes, and vice versa. It has also been shown that changes in the supply of money give rise to changes, in the same direction, in the equilibrium level of income.

As far as a fully employed economy is concerned, contractionary changes in any of the variables concerned lead to exactly the same effects as in an unemployed economy. However, expansionary changes cannot bring about increases in income when that variable is already at its maximum possible level. In such a case it is the price level that changes and, as we have seen, anything that shifts the *IS* curve to the right—an increase in government expenditure, a cut in taxes, or a shift of the investment function—will cause the price level to rise, while an increase in the money supply will actually lead to a proportionate increase in the price level.

These are important and interesting conclusions, for they suggest that fluctuations in the equilibrium level of income can be traced to disturbances in either the money market or the real-goods market. They also suggest that the three variables usually under government control—government expenditure, taxes, and the money supply—can be used to influence the equilibrium level of income or, at full employment, the equilibrium price level. Moreover, provided one knows the parameters of the model, the quantitative effects of such variations can be assessed (as will be apparent to the reader who works through the algebra in Appendix A).

Conclusions like these are neither better nor worse than the model upon which they are based and, if any parts of this model are suspect, so are these conclusions. If this were a treatise on macroeconomics, it would be instructive to take the pieces of the model one by one—the consumption function, the investment function, and so forth—and see how different hypotheses about their form alter the behavior of the model in which they are included. It would also be informative, where there are alternative hypotheses, to find out whether or not there is any way of sorting out the accurate and useful ones from those that may be misleading. However, the subject of this book is the demand function for money, and it is only this relationship that is treated in such a fashion. From now on, for purposes of exposition, it will be taken for granted that the formulations, set out above, of the consumption function and the investment function, to say nothing of the supply-of-money function, are sufficiently accurate as to not provide a misleading model. It is assumed that it is useful and empirically relevant to ask how various formulations of the demand-for-money function alter the behavior of such a model. The reader should, however, be just a little skeptical of the results presented in the next chapter, for he must remember that they depend upon the assumptions being made about the other functions in the model. With this caveat in mind, let us now turn to a discussion of the problems that differing assumptions about the demand-for-money function create in the context of this short-run macroeconomic model.

2

The Effects of Alternative Formulations of the Demand-for-Money Function

Alternative Specifications of the Demand-for-Money Function

The amount of faith that can be put in the conclusions stated in the preceding chapter about the effects of monetary and fiscal policy depends upon how much faith we are prepared to put in the model that yielded them. It was pointed out at the beginning of the last chapter that the accuracy and relevance of this model cannot be taken for granted. Even if we set aside any doubts we may have about the adequacy of the model's basic structure for dealing with all the problems with which we would like to deal, its behavior is still crucially dependent upon the specific assumptions we make about the particular functional relationships it contains.

There is a particularly acute problem so far as the demand-for-money function is concerned, because the available alternative formulations of this function are capable of radically changing the manner in which the whole model behaves. Two interrelated issues are particularly worth looking at. The first concerns the relationship between the demand for money and the rate of interest, and the other is the more general question of the stability of the relationship between the demand for money and the two variables upon which it was assumed to depend in the foregoing analysis. It is convenient to take up the matter of the rate of interest first.

It was assumed throughout the preceding chapter that the demand for money is stably and negatively related to the rate of interest, and this is a key assumption in the derivation of the upward sloping *LM* curve upon which so many of the conclusions drawn there rest. It has, however, been suggested by some economists that the demand for money is likely to be so insensitive to the rate of interest as to make it a reasonable approximation to treat it as not related to that variable at all. It has also been suggested, obviously by different economists, that, when the interest rate is very low relative to its normal level, the demand for money is so sensitive to the interest rate as to make it worthwhile to treat the relationship in question as being one of infinite elasticity.

This is not the place to go into the theoretical bases of these suggestions. They are taken up in Part II, but it is worthwhile now to look at the effects these different postulates have upon the behavior of our model. Figure 2-1 depicts demand functions for money drawn upon various assumptions concerning the role of the interest rate. Figure 2-1(a) reproduces the relevant figure from the previous chapter in which the relationship between the demand for money and the interest rate is assumed to be negative. Figure 2-1(b) should be almost self-explanatory. It is assumed here that there is no relationship between the demand for money and the rate of interest, but that the higher the level of income the greater the quantity of money demanded. The demand function becomes a series of vertical lines, those further to the right being associated with higher income levels. Figure 2-1(c) should not be any more difficult to interpret. It is assumed that at r^* the demand for money becomes completely elastic with respect to the rate of interest. At interest rates greater than r^* the demand for money increases with increases in income, but the curves drawn for different levels of income all converge and become perfectly elastic at r^*, since at this interest rate level increases in the level of income are not capable of causing an already unlimited demand for money to increase further.

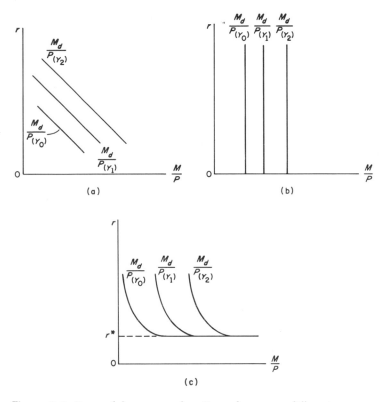

Figure 2-1. Demand-for-money functions drawn on different assumptions about the relationship between the demand for money and the rate of interest. $Y_2 > Y_1 > Y_0$.

Implications of the Alternatives with Unemployment

Let us now look at the implications of these hypotheses about the demand for money for the shape of the LM curve. The proposition that the demand for money is insensitive to the rate of interest implies that the LM curve is a vertical line, as shown in Figure 2-2(b), because the money market is in equilibrium when the demand for money is equal to its supply. This situation can occur at one and only one level of income for a given money supply if the demand for money is a continuously increasing function of that variable and depends on no other. The opposite extreme proposition about the relationship between the demand for money and the rate of interest—namely, that the relationship can be one of infinite rather than zero elasticity of

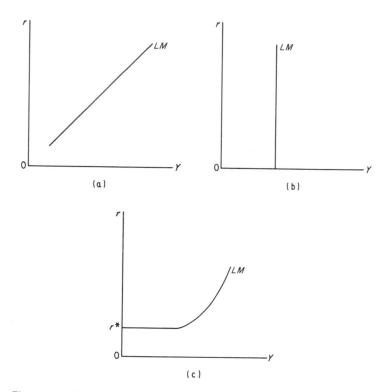

Figure 2-2. *LM* curves derived from the demand-for-money functions portrayed in Figure 2-1.

demand—produces an analogously opposite implication for the *LM* curve. Though it is positively sloped above *r**, it becomes horizontal at that level of the interest rate. This is shown in Figure 2-2(c), while Figure 2-2(a) reproduces the *LM* curve used in the previous chapter, so that the reader will have a basis for comparison.†

Given the *LM* curves that they imply, we can investigate the consequences for the behavior of the complete model of these various assumptions about the relationship between the demand for money and the rate of interest. Figure 2-3 deals with the effects of a shifting *IS* curve under conditions of unemployment equilibrium. As should

---

† The reader who has difficulty in seeing how to get from Figure 2-1 to Figure 2-2 should reproduce the former for himself, superimpose a given supply of money on it, and derive the *LM* curves in the manner followed in the previous chapter.

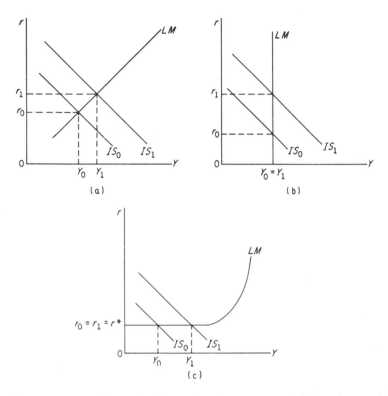

Figure 2-3. The effects of shifting the *IS* curve given different forms of the *LM* curve: unemployment.

be apparent, the results differ quite dramatically, depending upon what form the *LM* curve is assumed to take. In Figure 2-3(a) we present results from the previous chapter, which show that the level of income and the interest rate rise and fall together as the *IS* curve shifts. Figure 2-3(b) shows the results of assuming no relationship between the demand for money and the rate of interest. The only effect of shifting the *IS* curve in such a model is to raise and lower the rate of interest. On the other hand, Figure 2-3(c) shows that a horizontal *LM* curve involves all the resulting changes occurring in the level of income and none in the rate of interest.

Figure 2-4 deals with the consequences of shifting the *LM* curve, still in an unemployment situation. The case discussed in Chapter 1 is again displayed in Figure 2-4(a) for purposes of comparison, while Figure 2-4(b) shows that, when the demand for money is interest-

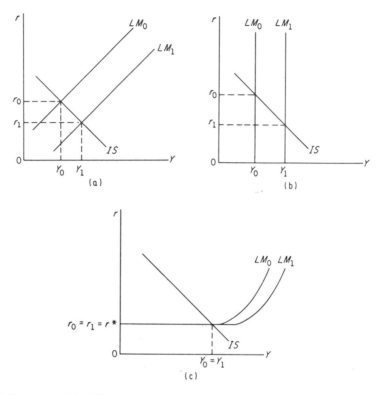

Figure 2-4. The effects of shifting LM curves of different forms: unemployment.

inelastic, shifts of the LM curve influence both the level of income and the rate of interest. The changes in both variables are greater than when there is some interest elasticity of demand for money, for a given shift of the LM curve to the right. When the demand for money is perfectly interest-elastic, we obtain what could be termed a curious result, for Figure 2-4(c) shows that, so long as one is operating in the region of the LM curve where the rate of interest is down to r^*, shifts in the curve alter neither the rate of interest nor the level of income.

Implications of the Alternatives at Full Employment

The mechanics of the model in a full-employment situation are dealt with in Figures 2-5 and 2-6, Figure 2-5 dealing with the consequences of shifting the IS curve. The results of the previous chapter, that a shift of the IS curve leads to a higher price level and a higher

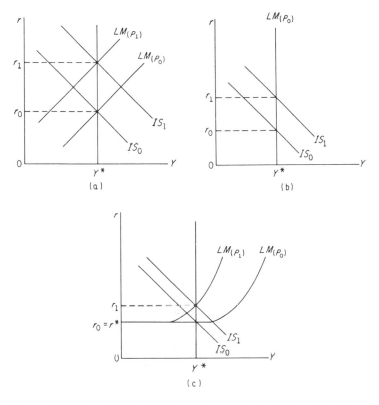

Figure 2-5. The effects at full employment of shifting the *IS* curve given (a) an upward sloping *LM* curve, (b) a vertical *LM* curve, and (c) an *LM* curve with a horizontal section. $P_1 > P_0$, but P_1 [panel (c)] is not equal to P_1 [panel (a)].

interest rate, no longer follow when the demand for money is assumed to be insensitive to the rate of interest. A higher interest rate is the only consequence of such a change, as Figure 2-5(b) shows. When the economy is in the region where the demand for money is perfectly interest-elastic at full employment, the result of a shift of the *IS* curve is ultimately a higher interest rate and a higher price level. The price level is higher by an indefinite amount, for it will continue to rise until the real-money supply has been so reduced in quantity as to permit the interest rate to rise above r^*, for at r^* there will always be excess demand in the economy once the *IS* curve has shifted.†

---

† This is, of course, a most unlikely case to come across in practice for it requires that the rate of interest needed to equilibrate the real-goods market at full employment be just equal to r^*. If this rate is less than r^* the economy will

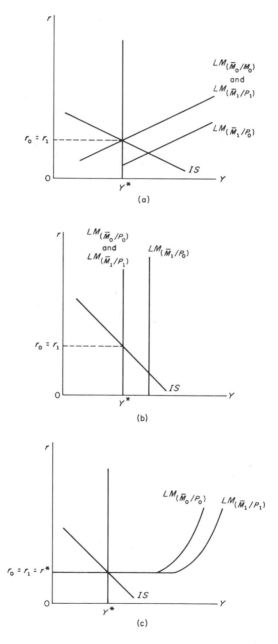

Figure 2-6. The effects of shifting LM curves of different forms: full employment. $M_1 > M_0$; $P_1 > P_0$.

Shifts in the *LM* curve are dealt with in Figure 2-6, and it is inter-esting to note that, at full employment, it makes no difference to the effects of a shift in the *LM* curve whether the demand for money is interest-elastic or not. In both Figures 2-6(a) and 2-6(b) it can be seen that, after a shift of the *LM* curve, the economy returns to equilibrium at the original level of the interest rate and at a higher price level, a price level that has in both cases risen in proportion to the change in the money supply that initially caused the *LM* curve to shift. It would of course make a difference if the *IS* curve shifted with the price level. (See footnote on p. 20.) The proportionality result would then hold only if the demand for money were totally interest-inelastic. In Figure 2-6(c) it is easy to see that, since shifting the *LM* curve to the right has no effect when the curve is horizontal, changing the supply of money can have no effect on the price level.†

Conclusions

In the last few pages we have mechanically worked through the consequences of differing assumptions about the nature of the rela-tionship between the demand for money and the rate of interest. The economic meaning of the results is easy to set out. We have seen that, if the demand for money is insensitive to the rate of interest, anything that shifts the *IS* curve will do nothing more than change the rate of interest—the equilibrium level of income (or, at full employment, the price level) being quite insensitive to such changes. This means that fluctuations in the equilibrium level of income in the economy can never be traced to fluctuations in the investment function. It also means that tax rates and government expenditure are quite useless as instruments for controlling the equilibrium level of economic activity. The quantity of money is the all-important variable in the model, the one that alone determines the equilibrium level of income in unemploy-ment situations and the equilibrium price level at full employment. In short, if the demand for money is interest-inelastic, fiscal policy is ineffective as an instrument of economic control, and monetary policy is all-powerful.

Just the opposite conclusions follow from the assumption that the demand for money is completely elastic with respect to the interest rate.

---

be in unemployment equilibrium and if it is above r^* the horizontal section of the *LM* curve will not be relevant to the equilibrium of the model. The case is then included more for the sake of taxonomic completeness than for its empirical relevance.

In this case, changes in the money stock are totally ineffective, and only factors that can shift the *IS* curve have any influence on either the level of income or the price level. Monetary policy is completely useless, and fiscal policy is all-powerful. In between these two extreme sets of results, it has also been shown that, if the demand for money is interest-elastic, but not perfectly so, both monetary and fiscal policy have a role to play in determining the equilibrium level of income— or, at full employment, the equilibrium price level.

The importance of the foregoing conclusions should be self-evident. Because it is such a vital issue for macroeconomics, the nature of the relationship between the demand for money and the rate of interest will receive much attention in the rest of this book.

One cannot illustrate quite so dramatically the importance of the other issues dealt with later in this volume, but they are important nevertheless. These issues involve the general problem of the stability of the demand-for-money function used here and in the previous chapter. Instability of this function can arise in at least three ways, all of which are worth mentioning.

First, it may be the case that, although the demand for money depends upon only the level of income and the rate of interest, this relationship is one that shifts randomly over time. If this is so, the *LM* curve will shift randomly over time as well and, given that the rest of the model is as specified earlier, this will lead to unexpected—not to mention unpredictable—fluctuations in the equilibrium level of income and employment, as well as perhaps in the price level. The knowledge that the demand-for-money function is subject to such random shifts is important not only for our understanding of economic history, but also for the manner in which we assess the likely efficacy of economic policies designed to control business fluctuations.

Second, instability in the relationship between the demand for money and the level of income and the rate of interest may be the result not of some random process but of some other variable (or variables) omitted from the function affecting the demand for money independently of the other relevant variables. As we shall see in the following chapters, there is no shortage of suggestions as to what these variables could be.

It is important to find out if any of them belong in the function, so that they can be incorporated fully in the model. Their potential effects on the behavior of the economy can then be investigated, thus enhancing our understanding of the way the macroeconomy works. Finally, it may be the case that the level of income is simply not relevant to the demand for money. Some economists, as we shall see, have suggested that wealth would be a more appropriate variable to use. This suggestion implies that the model we are dealing with is not properly specified, hence is likely to be misleading. Under such circumstances it would obviously be worthwhile to build an alternative model using the more relevant variable in the demand-for-money function. In addition to dealing with the specific nature of the relationship between the demand for money and the rate of interest, the following chapters also discuss the general stability of the demand-for-money function, trying to ascertain whether instability in the function is a result of relevant variables being omitted (or irrelevant variables being included) or whether the demand for money is subject to genuinely random fluctuations.

This by no means exhausts the list of problems with which the rest of this book deals, but it does indicate some of the key issues that arise in analyzing the role of the demand-for-money function in a macroeconomic context. The reader should at least be convinced that understanding the demand for money is well worth the effort.

Let us now turn to a discussion of the various theories about the demand for money that yield competing hypotheses about the nature of the function, leaving until Part III the assessment of the available empirical evidence on these matters.

A

The Algebra of the Model

Some readers may find it helpful to have the problems dealt with in Part I formulated in algebraic terms and all the results gathered together. If we restrict ourselves to linear functions for the sake of simplicity, we can write the model as follows, where Y is real national income, I is real investment, C is real consumption, M is money measured in nominal terms, P is price level, G is real government expenditure, T is real taxes, and r is rate of interest.

The consumption function:

$$C = A + c(Y - T) \tag{A-1}$$

The investment function:

$$I = B - ir \tag{A-2}$$

A proportional tax function:

$$T = tY \tag{A-3}$$

Government expenditure:

$$G = \bar{G} \tag{A-4}$$

The equilibrium condition for the goods market:

$$Y = C + \dot{I} + G \tag{A-5}$$

The demand-for-money function:

$$\frac{M_d}{P} = mY - Ir \tag{A-6}$$

The supply of money:

$$M_s = \bar{M}_s \tag{A-7}$$

The equilibrium condition for the money market:

$$M_s = M_d \tag{A-8}$$

Substituting Equations (A-1) through (A-4) into Equation (A-5), we have:

$$Y = A + B + G + c(1 - t)Y - ir \tag{A-9}$$

which can be rewritten as

$$r = \frac{1}{i}(A + B + \bar{G}) - \frac{1 - c(1 - t)}{i}Y \tag{A-10}$$

This is the *IS* curve. We can also substitute Equations (A-6) and (A-7) into Equation (A-8) to obtain

$$r = \frac{1}{I}\frac{\bar{M}_s}{P} + \frac{m}{I}Y \tag{A-11}$$

This is the *LM* curve. Equating the right-hand sides of Equations (A-10) and (A-11) we can write

$$-\frac{1}{I}\frac{\bar{M}_s}{P} + \frac{m}{I}Y = \frac{1}{i}(A + B + \bar{G}) - \frac{1 - c(1 - t)}{i}Y \tag{A-12}$$

There are two unknowns in Equation (A-12), the level of income and the price level. However, if it is assumed that the price level can be taken as fixed and given in unemployment situations and, if we regard some level of income as being uniquely associated with full employment, Equation (A-12) can be rearranged to yield one expression to determine the level of income in unemployment situations and another to determine the level of prices at full employment. Where P^* is the given price level and Y^* is full-employment income, these expressions are

$$Y = \frac{1}{1 - c(1-t) + (i/l)m}(A+B+\bar{G}) + \frac{1}{m + (l/i)[1 - c(1-t)]}\frac{\bar{M}_s}{P^*}$$

$$(A\text{-}13)$$

and

$$P = \frac{1}{Y^*\{m + (l/i)[1 - c(1-t)]\} - (l/i)(A+B+\bar{G})}\bar{M}_s \quad (A\text{-}14)$$

If we wish to investigate the effects of changes in such variables as the level of government expenditure, the tax rate, and the supply of money on the level of income in unemployment situations, or indeed at full employment when the changes in question are contractionary ones, we need only take the partial derivative of Equation (A-13) with respect to the appropriate variable. The effect of expansionary changes at full employment can be investigated by performing similar operations on Equation (A-14). If we do this, we obtain, when there is unemployment,

$$\frac{\delta Y}{\delta G} = \frac{1}{(i/l)m + [1 - c(1-t)]} > 0 \quad (A\text{-}15)$$

$$\frac{\delta Y}{\delta t} = -cY\frac{1}{(i/l)m + [1 - c(1-t)]} < 0 \quad (A\text{-}16)$$

$$\frac{\delta Y}{\delta \bar{M}_s} = \frac{1}{(m + (l/i)[1 - c(1 - c(1-t))]\}P^*} \quad (A\text{-}17)$$

and, at full employment,

$$\frac{\delta P}{\delta \bar{G}} = \frac{P^2}{M_s}\frac{l}{i} > 0 \quad (A\text{-}18)$$

$$\frac{\delta P}{\delta t} = -cY\frac{P^2}{M_s}\frac{l}{i} < 0 \qquad \text{(A-19)}$$

$$\frac{\delta P}{\delta \overline{M}_s} = \frac{1}{Y^*\{m + (l/i)[1 - c(1-t)]\} - (l/i)(A+B+\overline{G})} > 0 \quad \text{(A-20)}$$

These equations tell us that, at less than full employment, increasing government expenditure, cutting the tax rate, and increasing the money supply will all lead to a higher equilibrium level of income, while at full employment similar policies will lead to increases in the equilibrium price level. Equation (A-20) also tells us that changes in the price level are proportional to changes in the quantity of money.

Equations (A-15) through (A-20) can be used to illustrate the specific problems concerning the role of the rate of interest in the demand-for-money function dealt with in Chapter 2. The less sensitive the demand for money to the rate of interest the closer to zero the value of l, the parameter linking these variables, while the more sensitive the relationship in question the closer this parameter approaches infinity.

It should be clear from inspection of Equations (A-15) through (A-20) that, as l approaches 0, so do Equations (A-15), (A-16), (A-18), and (A-19), while Equation (A-17) approaches $1/m$ and Equation (A-20) approaches $1/Y^*m$. It should be equally clear that, as l approaches infinity, so do Equations (A-18) and (A-19), while Equations (A-17) and (A-20) approach zero. Equation (A-15) approaches

$$\frac{1}{1 - c(1-t)}$$

and Equation (A-16) goes to

$$-cY\frac{1}{1 - c(1-t)}$$

That is to say, the less sensitive the demand for money to the rate of interest, the less effective fiscal policy becomes and the more exclusively the level of income or the price level comes to depend upon the quantity of money. However, the more sensitive the demand for money is to these variables, the less relevant the money market is in determining the way in which income and prices react to policy changes, and the more influence must be accorded fiscal policy. One must be a little careful in interpreting the approach of Equations (A-18) and (A-19) to infinity as l approaches infinity. This means that, so long as the demand for money remains perfectly elastic with respect to the rate of interest, the price level will rise without limit after an expansionary fiscal policy undertaken at full employment. It is precisely the fact that this region of the demand-for-money function becomes irrelevant as the price level rises that stops the price rise from going on forever. The rise in price in question is indefinite rather than infinite. However, the whole issue concerns a most unlikely set of circumstances as noted above. (See footnote on p. 31.) The other set of problems dealt with at the end of Chapter 2 concern with the stability of the parameters m and l, and inspection of Equations (A-13) and (A-14) should convince the reader that, if these parameters are not stable or predictable, neither is the price level or the level of income.

Finally, the reader should note that the value of the parameter i is every bit as crucial for the behavior of this model as that of l. If i goes to zero, this has the same effect on the model, as far as income and price level determination are concerned, as l going to infinity. i measures the sensitivity of investment to the rate of interest. Because of the crucial role this parameter plays in the behavior of the macro model under analysis here, the role of interest rates in determining investment, and other, expenditures, has attracted much attention from investigators doing empirical work in macroeconomics. It is beyond the scope of this book to deal with the issues considered in that work, but the reader should be in no doubt about their importance to macroeconomics.

B

The Wealth Effect

As noted in Chapter 1, the wealth effect is a mechanism whereby changes in the price level shift the *IS* curve. They change the level of aggregate demand directly, rather than by way of their effect on interest rates. The basic hypothesis about behavior underlying the mechanism is that consumption, in addition to depending upon income, also depends upon the real value of the stock of assets held in the economy. The greater the stock of wealth the higher consumption. If the stock of wealth varies inversely with the price level, so will consumption.

The wealth-effect mechanism was first introduced into macroeconomics as a means of showing that, if prices are flexible downward, even when the minimum interest rate permitted by a horizontal *LM* curve is above that required for full-employment aggregate demand as given on the *IS* curve, the economy will still reach full-employment equilibrium eventually; the wealth effect will keep the *IS* curve shifting to the right so long as prices fall, and prices will fall until full employment is reached. Since its introduction in connection with this particular problem, the wealth-effect mechanism has attracted much analytic attention, and several elegant, not to mention illuminating, models of both micro- and macroeconomic behavior have been built around it, particularly by Patinkin (1965).

For the wealth effect to operate it is necessary that the stock of real wealth vary with the price level. The real value of equity capital is clearly independent of the price level, since it is a physical stock of goods. Moreover, though individuals may issue to one another bonds denominated in units of current purchasing power, bonds whose real value changes when the price level changes, these make no difference to the overall position in the economy, since the wealth of debtors and creditors moves equally and oppositely when the price level changes. So long as there are no effects of changes in the distribution of wealth, privately issued bonds are irrelevant so far as the wealth effect is concerned. Its operation seems to require that some of the economy's assets, denominated in nominal terms, be the debt of no one in the economy. If such assets exist, a rise in the price level will make their holders worse off without making anyone else correspondingly better off by diminishing his real indebtedness. A fall in the price level will make their owners better off, at the expense of no one.

It is sometimes argued that government debt, including that part of the money supply that represents the liability of the government rather than of a privately owned banking system, represents such an asset, since it is owned by the private sector of the economy yet represents the debt of no one in the private sector. If we accept this argument for the moment, it will be clear that a fall in the price level will involve a rise in the real value of the government debt, a consequent rise in the value of the overall level of wealth in the economy, hence a rise in the level of consumption expenditure.

However, it is generally agreed that it is too simplistic to treat the full value of interest-bearing government debt as net wealth to the private sector of the economy. Interest payments on such debt have to be met by taxes levied on the private sector. If people in the private sector realize this, an increase in the real value of government debt outstanding will also involve an increase in the present value of future tax liabilities. However, there is some reason to argue that these two influences will not completely cancel each other out. Government securities are easily marketable assets which, moreover, can be bequeathed to one's heirs. Tax liabilities are not bequeathed specifically to one's heirs. Also, to the extent that taxes are levied on labor income—which can be regarded as a return to a nonmarketable asset called human capital—the effect of increasing the real value of government debt outstanding, and financing the increased interest payments out of taxes, is to convert some of the return to a nonmarketable asset into a return on a marketable security. If marketability enhances the value of an asset, an increase in the real value of government debt outstanding represents some increase in the community's wealth, although not by the full amount of the increase in the value of the debt.

Non-interest-bearing government debt, however, can be treated as net wealth in its full amount. This is because an increase in the real value of such debt outstanding carries with it no corresponding increase in tax liabilities. The same is true, however, of non-interest-bearing private debt, not just of public debt. Suppose a private bank holds interest-bearing securities denominated in units of current purchasing power as its assets, but that its corresponding liabilities are non-interest-bearing demand deposits. In this case, a fall in the price level will increase the real value of the bank's interest income but leave the real value of its interest payments constant at zero. A fall in the price level thus enhances the profitability of the bank, hence the wealth of its owners, while the rise in the wealth of its depositors is just offset by the fall in the wealth of the bank's debtors. If instead of nominal assets the bank held equity, we would find an increase in wealth accruing to its depositors, no change in the real value of the bank's assets, hence no change in the real liabilities of its debtors. Once more there would be an increase in the community's net wealth, but this time accruing to the bank's customers rather than to its owners.

The foregoing analysis stems from the debate that followed the publication of Pesek and Saving (1967) and draws in particular on Johnson (1969) and Laidler (1969). If it is correct, and the matter is ultimately an empirical one, it is appropriate to treat non-interest-bearing money and perhaps some, in the present state of knowledge unspecified, proportion of interest-bearing government debt as net wealth to the private sector of the economy. Hence there is certainly some interdependence between the behavior of the price level and the IS curve, which is not captured by the analysis carried out earlier. For some macroeconomic issues—such as those dealt with by Patinkin and alluded to above—this is an important matter; but for our purposes, which involve assessing the significance of alternative formulations of the demand-for-money function for the behavior of the economy, the extra analytic simplicity gained by ignoring the wealth effect seems well worth the associated sacrifice of analytic precision.

THEORIES OF THE DEMAND FOR MONEY

CHAPTER

3

A Brief Overview

The statement that the demand for money measured in real terms depends upon the level of real national income and the rate of interest is a particular hypothesis about the nature of the demand function for money. The issues raised in Chapter 2 amount to asking how good a hypothesis it is. At first sight this is a question that can be answered by immediate reference to empirical evidence, for it seems reasonable to suppose that one could ask how much of the variation in the quantity of money demanded in any particular economy can be explained by reference to variations in these variables. This can of course be done, but before embarking upon such an empirical study one should ask in advance what conclusions could be drawn from the results to be obtained.

If it were to turn out that all the variations in the demand for money could be explained by the variables in question, it might be concluded that the theory was a perfect one. At the other extreme, if these variables turned out to explain nothing at all, the theory might be judged perfectly useless.† Neither of these outcomes is very likely; more probably the theory will turn out to explain 50% or 90% of the variation in the demand for money, and whether a theory that can explain 90% of the variation in the demand for money is good or bad is not a question that can be sensibly answered. It all depends on how one defines "good" and "bad."

Provided there is no difference between them in terms of scope, logical simplicity, or consistency with other economic models and such, one can say that a theory that explains 90% of the variation in the demand for money is *better* than one that explains 50%. If there are several alternative theories involved, one can pick the best of them on the basis of a criterion such as this, for so long as it also satisfies the other criteria mentioned above, a theory is good if it passes empirical tests better than some other theory, and bad if it fails to do so. If one wishes to learn about economic theory by referring to empirical evidence, one will need not one but several hypotheses that can be put to the test simultaneously, for it is only in this way that useful theoretical ideas can be sorted out from those that are misleading.

The lesson here for the problem of the demand for money is that it is not possible to learn much about the empirical relevance of the proposition that the demand for money depends stably and predictably on the level of income and the rate of interest until the predictions that follow from this proposition are compared with those that follow from other, different, hypotheses about the variables upon which the demand for money depends. As we shall see in the next few chapters, there is no shortage of alternative theories and, as we shall also see, what we know about the empirical nature of the demand-for-money function has been learned from tests that sought to compare the performance of such competing hypotheses. It is useful, then, to go over the various theories in some detail before going on to consider any empirical evidence.

It may strike the reader as strange that one should talk about the theory of the demand for money at all. This is not the economist's usual approach to such problems. Textbooks of microeconomics do not contain chapters with titles like "The Theory of the Demand for

† But "all the variation" implies that one has all the relevant evidence. Since such evidence is continually being generated, one never has all of it, and the notion of a theory being completely verified by the evidence is totally irrelevant to scientific procedure. Even if a theory is found that explains all available evidence perfectly, there is always the possibility that new evidence, incompatible with the theory in question, may turn up.

Refrigerators," but rather present a generalized analytic framework in terms of which the demand for any good can be treated. Though there is now a substantial body of literature that deals with the demand for money as merely a special case of the general theory of demand, it was only in the 1950s that this approach received a clear and influential statement.† Before then, and even now to a great extent, the demand for money was usually treated as a case apart needing separate analysis, and persuasive reasons for doing this are not hard to find. The usual approach to demand theory is to postulate that an individual consumer receives satisfaction from the consumption of various goods, and that it is from this satisfaction, usually called *utility*, that his market demand for goods and services derives. In the case of durable goods, there is an intermediate step, for the demand for a *stock* of durable goods is derived from the utility the consumer receives from the *flow* of services they provide. Usually, the nature of the utility function involved is dismissed as the business of psychology and, apart from some very general assumption about its nature, involving the principle of the diminishing marginal rate of substitution between goods in consumption, it is not investigated by economists.

Now, money does not seem to fit very well into this framework. It is not something that is physically consumed, nor does it, like other consumer durable goods, seem to yield a flow of services that give psychological satisfaction to an individual. It does not keep food fresh as does a refrigerator, or provide entertainment as does a television set. Stocks and bonds are in the same category, but they yield their owners a cash income which may be spent on consumption goods, and money generally speaking does not do this. In some economies, a small interest income is to be had from assets that are also used as money, but the desire to hold cash cannot be explained by this fact. There are many instances of money yielding no interest and being held nevertheless. It may look, then, as if utility theory cannot be used as a direct explanation as to why money is held, so that the demand for it must be treated as a special case.

Two peculiar and interrelated characteristics of money are usually emphasized in theories that set it apart from other goods. The first is that money is acceptable as a means of exchange for goods and services, and the second is that its market value is generally highly pre-

---

† Though the potential of this method was clearly enough set out 4 decades ago by Hicks (1935).

dictable. These two characteristics, which are usually collectively called *liquidity*, are not the exclusive property of money. Other assets also possess them in varying degrees.

In some cases it may be possible to convince the seller of a good to accept some other item in exchange for it; furthermore, the prices of some assets are quite predictable and fluctuate little. Thus sellers of new automobiles are willing to accept used vehicles as trade-ins, and the existence of a well-developed used car market makes the trade-in price of a particular vehicle at a particular time relatively easy to predict. However, unlike such assets as used cars, money is *universally* acceptable as a means of exchange, and its value is usually more predictable than that of other assets. Money is the most liquid of assets, and it is argued that there are two reasons why this leads to its being demanded.

When transactions are undertaken, it is clearly necessary to have money on hand with which to make payments, but this fact alone is not a sufficient explanation of why money is held. In a perfectly frictionless world, an individual would buy an income-earning asset the moment he received a payment, selling it again only the very moment he required money to make a payment on his own account. He would thus never hold money. However, the world is not frictionless; purchases and sales of assets take time and trouble and hence are not costless. Also, it is far from clear that an income-earning asset can be sold at any particular moment at the price for which it was bought. There is an element of uncertainty involved here and, though gains are to be made by holding such assets, so are losses. Costs and losses alike can be avoided by bridging the gap between the receipt of payments and the making of expenditures by holding money rather than other assets.

Closely related to this argument is the fact that no individual can be completely certain about when it is that he will be involved in acts of buying and selling goods and services. Thus he can never be quite sure that his current receipts will match his current planned expenditures at every moment. Again, this would not matter in a perfectly frictionless world but, where it is costly to exchange income-earning assets for money, it pays an individual to keep money on hand in order to acquire extra flexibility for his market activities. Because of the costs involved in buying and selling income-earning assets, because the price of such assets can be uncertain, because the timing of some market transactions is also uncertain, and because money is readily acceptable in any transaction, it comes to be held. Notions such as these form the basis of a great deal of theorizing about the demand for money.

The use of money in transactions is not the only factor from which a demand for it is derived, for its predictable market value can make it a desirable asset to hold. One earns no income, or only a relatively small one if money does bear interest, from holding money, so that other assets are normally a preferable way of holding wealth, but normally is not quite the same thing as invariably. From time to time, expectations about future fluctuations in the prices of income-earning assets may lead wealth holders to believe that to own them will lead to capital losses. A zero gain from holding money at such times is clearly preferable to a loss from holding other assets, so that, quite apart from its use in transactions, money becomes something desirable to hold. Analysis of this type of behavior is also quite prominent in theorizing about the demand for money.

In the last few paragraphs we have argued that money indeed performs important services for its owners, even if such services are not of the kind that yield psychological satisfaction. Since, however, it has never proved necessary to investigate the nature of the psychological satisfaction that arises from the consumption of other goods in order to analyze the demand for them, it can well be argued that the psychological overtones with which utility theory is invested are irrelevant to it. Certain approaches to the theory of demand take this position. If one adopts such a view, the fact that the services of money are not psychological becomes irrelevant in applying utility theory to the problem of the demand for it. It becomes sufficient to postulate that money yields services to its owner, and then to analyze the determinants of the demand for money in the same way one would for any other good. Whether this is a sensible approach or not is best judged by the predictive power of the theory that emerges from it rather than by philosophical discussions of its underlying assumptions.

Theories of the demand for money based on an application of the general theory of demand are not logically incompatible with the notion that the demand for money in fact arises from its usefulness in making transactions or with the proposition that it is an excellent hedge against the risk inherent in holding other assets. Nor are the latter two approaches contradictory to one another. However, theories that stress the importance of transactions lead to different models of the demand for money than those that stress the uncertainty involved in holding other assets. An approach that deliberately avoids any analysis of motivation and simply applies generalized notions about the determination of the demand for any good to the demand for money leads to yet a different model.

These various models could be regarded as all forming part of one general theory of the demand for money, but it is methodologically convenient to treat them as alternatives and then to ask how much of the variation in the demand for money is to be explained solely by the factors that each particular hypothesis suggests are important. If it should be the case that no one set of variables dominates the demand-for-money function, one will find this out from the results of his experiments but, if one particular set of variables does dominate the scene he will also discover this from such a procedure, and information of this character would be of particular interest. The more one can explain with fewer variables, the simpler, hence more manageable and easy to understand, will be the theory that emerges from such work. As a matter of method, then, rather than as a matter of strict logic, the theories presented in subsequent chapters are stated so that the differences rather than the similarities between them are emphasized, so that they appear as alternative rather than complementary models. Only by treating them in this way will it be possible later to state clearly the issues that have been dealt with in recent empirical work.

CHAPTER

4

The Classics, Keynes, and the Modern Quantity Theory

Irving Fisher's Version of the Quantity Theory

One of the most complete, as well as influential, pieces of analysis based on the role of money as a means of exchange did not explicitly formulate the problem in the framework of a theory of demand though, as we shall see, the results are readily transformed into such terms. Rather than the demand for money, the concept emphasized was the transactions velocity of circulation of money, the rate at which it passes from hand to hand. Irving Fisher (1911), who is the economist most closely associated with this approach, began his analysis with a simple identity.

In every transaction there is both a buyer and a seller, hence for the aggregate economy the value of sales must equal the value of receipts. Now the value of sales must be equal to the number of transactions conducted over any time period multiplied by the average price at which they take place. However, the value of purchases must be equal to the amount of money in circulation in the economy times the average number of times it changes hands over the same time period. Hence, where M_s is the quantity of money, V_T is the number of times it turns over, its transactions velocity of circulation, P is the price level, and T is the volume of transactions, one can write, as an identity

$$M_s V_T \equiv PT \tag{4-1}$$

Nothing follows from an identity except another identity, but it can be used as a classificatory device in the process of theory building; one can consider the four variables listed above and ask what it is that determines their values. Fisher's answers were as follows. The quantity of money is determined independently of any of the three other variables and at any time can be taken as given. Moreover, T, the volume of transactions, can also be taken as given. In an economy that has its only equilibrium at full-employment levels of income, and Fisher in company with nearly all his contemporaries held this view, it seems reasonable to assume that there is a certain fixed ratio of the volume of transactions to the level of output. Fisher also treated V_T as a variable independent of the others in the identity, and, although he did not regard it as being a constant at each and every moment in time, he did view it as taking a constant equilibrium value to which it quickly returned after any disturbance. Thus the equilibrium value of the final variable P is determined by the interaction of the other three.

More specifically, if T and the equilibrium value of V_T are taken as constants, we arrive at the proposition that the equilibrium price level is determined solely by, and is proportional to, the quantity of money. These further assumptions permit us to translate our identity, the *equation of exchange*, into the *quantity theory of money*, a theory of the determination of the price level, which can be written

$$M_s \bar{V}_T = P\bar{T} \tag{4-2}$$

with the bars over V and T signifying that they are constants.

Though not stated as such by Fisher, this is equivalent to the following theory of the money market put in supply and demand terms. The demand for money depends upon the value of the transactions to be conducted in the economy and is equal to a constant fraction of these transactions. Furthermore, the supply of money is given, and in equilibrium the demand for money must be equal to its supply. This can be written

$$M_d = k_T P \overline{T} \tag{4-3}$$

$$M_d = M_s \tag{4-4}$$

and these two equations can be combined to deduce that

$$M_s \frac{1}{k_T} = M_s \overline{V}_T = P\overline{T} \tag{4-5}$$

where

$$\overline{V}_T \equiv \frac{1}{k_T} \tag{4-6}$$

Whether one puts this approach in terms of velocity or in terms of a demand function linking money balances to the volume of transactions in an economy, one still has to ask the question, what determines velocity or the equilibrium money/transactions ratio? The answer given is cast in largely technological terms. Once it has been argued that the demand for money stems from its use in the transactions-making process, it is but a short step to saying that the exact amount of money normally needed to carry out any given volume of transactions is determined by the nature of this process as it exists in any particular economy. There is an underlying analogy here with the analysis of a production process, the volume of transactions playing the role of the output and money that of an input.

Once the matter is posed this way, theorizing about the demand for money inevitably begins to concentrate on the nature of this production process. The institutional arrangements surrounding the settlement of accounts come in for study. To give one example, it appears that an economy in which the use of credit cards is widespread would need less money to finance a given volume of business than one in which all payments must be made directly in cash. For similar reasons, the practices of businesses with regard to granting one another trade credit attracts attention. On another level, the quality of communications in an economy appears important. The fact that funds can be transmitted by telephone or telegraph should lead to a smaller requirement for money than there would be in an economy in which all messages must be sent by mail. One could list such examples as these almost without end, but enough has been said here to give the reader the flavor of this approach to the theory of the demand for money.

The important thing about this view, for our purposes, is that factors such as credit practices, communications, and so on, though they can certainly change over time, do not alter rapidly. Thus if one thinks of them as being the principal determinants of the demand for money in an economy, it can be argued that, over short time periods, there is little scope for variation in the amount of money demanded relative to the volume of transactions being conducted. He would thus expect the velocity of circulation to be stable over such periods and, taking a longer view, would expect changes in velocity to be rather slow and drawn out, responding to slow institutional changes. Thus, as a good short-run approximation, the transactions velocity of circulation is treated as a constant.

Furthermore, it is also tempting to look at the relationship between the volume of transactions and the level of national income in this way, depending as the former does on such matters as the number of stages goods go through between the raw material and the final product stage, and the number of independent firms involved. Though vertical integration of industries can certainly take place and cut down on the volume of transactions associated with any given level of output, it is not likely to be a rapid process. Hence it can be ignored for the purposes of short-run analysis—or so it tends to be asserted in this type of approach to monetary theory. Similarly, the proportion of national income actually involved in market transactions can change over time as economic units become more and more specialized and hence interdependent, producing less and less for their own consumption and more and more for the market. Again though, a change such as this is not likely to be a rapid one and can perhaps be ignored for short-run purposes.†

This transactions approach to monetary theory, then, tends to lead to the hypothesis that the demand for money is a constant proportion of the level of transactions, which in turn bears a constant relationship to the level of national income. Moreover, though when the theory was first propounded there was an assumption that full-employment income was the only equilibrium for the economy, full employment is not an essential part of the theory. We can easily drop this assumption, fit this theory of the behavior of the money market

---

† This whole line of reasoning, however, overlooks the large and rapid fluctuations that can take place in the volume of transactions conducted in financial markets.

into a general macroeconomic framework, and ask what the resulting model implies.

If the demand for money depends only upon the level of income and prices, we have the special case of the general model, developed in Part I, in which, because the demand for money is independent of the rate of interest, the level of real income, or at full employment the price level, depends solely upon the size of the money supply. Whether or not this particular approach to monetary theory leads to correct conclusions is a moot point, but it cannot be denied that it leads to interesting conclusions which, if they turn out to be correct, have very important implications for the way in which governments should carry out economic policy. It implies nothing less than that the equilibrium level of income, or prices at full employment, cannot be influenced in any way by fiscal policy. It is thus a piece of analysis to be taken very seriously and to be tested with great care.

The Cambridge Approach

Fisher's approach to monetary economics has much to recommend it, for, by postulating that the demand for money arises as a result of the need of individuals to trade with one another, it links the demand for money to the volume of trade going on in an economy at any time, hence leads directly to a macroeconomic theory of the demand for money; it also leads to fairly precise predictions about the nature of the demand-for-money function, hence is eminently testable. None of this, though, is a logically necessary consequence of analyzing the demand for money from the point of view of the role it plays in the transactions-making process, for, as we shall now see, the Cambridge approach to the problem of the demand for money, as epitomized in the work of Marshall and Pigou, although it starts in the same place and ends with a formal statement of the demand-for-money function that looks very similar to the one that follows from a Fisher approach, follows a totally different path to get there, as the reader of Pigou (1917) soon discovers.

The Cambridge economists did not ask, as Fisher did, what determines the amount of money an economy needs to carry out a given volume of transactions, but rather what determines the amount of money an individual would wish to hold given that the desire to conduct transactions makes money holding desirable at all. Thus the question was put in microeconomic terms and laid emphasis on the choice-making behavior of individuals. This approach is much more akin to an application of the general theory of demand to a particular problem than it is to a special theory of the demand for money, and, when the problem is cast in these terms, the kinds of variables an economist is led to look at tend to be different from those to which Fisher's approach points.

essence

If one considers the problem as one involving the amount of money an individual chooses to hold, the framework that suggests itself is one in which constraints and opportunity costs are the central factors, interacting with individuals' tastes. As far as the Cambridge approach is concerned, the principal determinant of people's "taste" for money holding is the fact that it is a convenient asset to have, being universally acceptable in exchange for goods and services. The more transactions an individual has to undertake the more cash he will want to hold. To this extent the approach is similar to Fisher's, but the emphasis is on *want* to hold, rather than *have* to hold. This is the basic difference between Cambridge monetary theory and the Fisher framework.

An individual cannot hold all the money he wants, if only because his stock of cash balances cannot exceed his total wealth. This is the constraint upon his money holding. Moreover, even if it were possible for a person to have all his wealth in the form of money, it is far from clear that this would be what he would desire. There are alternative ways of holding assets, and many of them offer advantages that money does not offer. Stocks and bonds offer an interest income that money does not and, if it is posited that the more money held the less the convenience to be gained from holding yet more of it, it becomes clear that after a point it will prove preferable to sacrifice some of this convenience in order to have some interest income. Moreover, stock and bond holding brings with it a chance for making capital gains (or losses), as indeed does money holding in times of a fluctuating price level, and one expects anyone deciding how to allocate his wealth to take such matters into account before deciding on how much of it to devote to money balances.

All this is to say that the demand for money, in addition to depending upon the volume of transactions an individual may be planning to conduct, also varies with the level of his wealth, and with the opportunity cost of holding money, the income forgone by not holding other assets. If we are talking about money measured in nominal terms, it also varies exactly in proportion to the price level. This is because the convenience of holding money derives from its usefulness in carrying out the transactions necessary to obtain goods and services. If the prices of these things were to increase by a certain proportion, the quantity of money an individual would have to hold in order to achieve just the same convenience as before would also have to increase by the same proportion.

We have not explicitly mentioned factors such as the availability of money substitutes for making transactions, the availability of good communications, and so on (the items stressed by the Fisher approach), but it should be clear that these can hardly be excluded from this scheme; they must, in part at least, determine the degree to which it is convenient to hold money rather than other assets at any given time. However, these matters are given a subservient position in the Cambridge analysis of the problem of the demand for money.

The Cambridge approach to the theory of the demand for money amounts to saying that, if one looks at the problem of money holding in an economy from the point of view of individual choice-making behavior, one will consider the convenience an individual derives from money holding for the making of transactions, his wealth, the rate of interest, the expectations he holds about the future course of events, and so on, as being potentially important influences upon the demand for money. It says little about the nature of the relationships one can expect to prevail between these variables, and it does not say too much about which ones are important. Rather, when formalizing their model, this group of economists, particularly Pigou, chose to simplify it by assuming that for an individual the level of wealth, the volume of transactions, and the level of income are—over short periods at least—in stable proportions to one another. They then argued that, other things being equal, the demand for money in nominal terms is proportional to the nominal level of income for each individual, hence for the aggregate economy as well. Thus they wrote the demand equation for money:

$$M_d = kPY \tag{4-7}$$

which, combined with an equilibrium condition for the money market,

$$M_d = M_s \tag{4-4}$$

gives

$$M_s = kPY \tag{4-8}$$

hence

$$M_s \frac{1}{k} = M_s V = PY \tag{4-9}$$

which looks very similar to Fisher's approach, except that V represents not the *transactions* velocity of circulation of money, referred to above as V_T, but rather its *income* velocity—not the number of times a unit of money physically turns over, but rather its rate of circulation relative to the rate of production of real income.

Taken in these terms, then, the Cambridge approach appears to lead to a model of the money market similar to Fisher's and seems to yield the same implications for the roles of monetary policy and fiscal policy in controlling the level of income. To give it this interpretation though would be a mistake. Both Fisher and the Cambridge economists stated their theories on an other-things-being-equal basis. What Fisher required to be constant, the institutional framework determining the technical nature of the transactions-making process, may reasonably be expected not to change perceptibly over short periods; hence his approach can be regarded as providing a theory of the money market that implies a constant equilibrium velocity of circulation in the short run. Not so with the Cambridge economists with their emphasis on the rate of interest and expectations, for these are variables one can expect to vary significantly over quite short periods.

To state Marshall and Pigou's model in a manner that makes it look like Fisher's is to hide important differences between the formulations, and to ignore the fact that the Cambridge approach, above all, calls for further analysis of the variables involved before stating a formal theory of the money market based on it. In terms of the macroeconomic model presented in the last chapter, some economists have suggested that Fisher has propounded a hypothesis that the rate of interest has no significant effect on the demand for money. There is room for debate about the appropriateness of interpreting Fisher in this way but, in any event, it is more difficult to derive so definite a proposition from the work of Marshall and Pigou. Although the formal version of the Cambridge demand-for-money function does not include an interest rate variable, it is nevertheless true that one of the main contributions of the Cambridge school to monetary theory was to call attention to the fact that such variables as the rate of interest may be important determinants of the demand for money.

They left it to their successors, however, to investigate their suggestions in detail.

The Keynesian Theory

It is Keynes's (1936) development of the Cambridge approach to the problem of the demand for money that now forms the basis of the treatment of the subject in macroeconomics textbooks.† He analyzed with more care than his predecessors the motives that lead people to hold money and as a result was more precise than they on the nature of the convenience to be had from its possession. As we have seen, the peculiar characteristic of money as an asset that was emphasized by Fisher and the Cambridge school alike was the fact that money, alone among assets, is universally acceptable as a means of exchange. Keynes by no means rejected this point of view, and indeed listed the "transactions motive" as the first—but by no means only—motive he recognized as underlying the demand for money.

He postulated, perhaps more clearly than those who had written before him, that the level of transactions conducted by an individual, and also by the aggregate of individuals, bears a stable relationship to the level of income, and hence that the "transactions demand" for money is proportional to the level of income. There is nothing new in this aspect of the Keynesian approach. The use of the term "transactions motive," though, was confined to describing the necessity of holding cash to bridge the gap between receipts and planned regular payments. For those classes of payments that cannot be considered regular and planned, such as paying unexpected bills, making purchases at unexpectedly favorable prices, meeting sudden emergencies caused perhaps by accidents or ill health, he also suggested that people find it prudent to hold some cash in case they are not able to realize other assets quickly enough to be of use to them. This he called the "precautionary motive" for holding money and suggested that the demand for money arising from it also depends, by and large, on the level of income.

† The distinction between the Cambridge approach and the work of Keynes is a somewhat arbitrary one. *A Tract on Monetary Reform* (Keynes, 1923) is completely within the tradition of Marshall and Pigou, as are those sections of *A Treatise on Money* (Keynes, 1930) dealing explicitly with the demand for money, though the general frame of reference of this work is Wicksellian dynamics. It is only in *The General Theory of Employment, Interest, and Money* (Keynes, 1936) that we find what is now referred to as Keynesian monetary theory.

Keynes himself was not willing to regard the demand for money arising from the transactions motive and the precautionary motive as being in some sense technically fixed in its relationship to the level of income, for he saw quite clearly that the convenience to be had from holding cash for these purposes can be traded off against the return from holding other assets. He made the transactions and precautionary demands for money functions of the rate of interest. However, he did not stress the role of the rate of interest in this part of his analysis, and many of his popularizers ignored it altogether, not because the rate of interest is not important in Keynes's analysis, but because its chief importance is to be found in the role it plays in determining the "speculative demand" for money.†

Marshall and Pigou had suggested that uncertainty about the future was one of the factors that can be expected to influence the demand for money, and Keynes's analysis of the speculative motive represents an attempt to formalize one aspect of this suggestion and to draw conclusions from it. Rather than talk of uncertainty in general, the field is narrowed to uncertainty about one economic variable—the future level of the rate of interest—in the following manner.

A bond is an asset that carries with it the promise to pay its owner a certain income per annum, fixed in money terms, and the decision to buy a bond is a decision to buy a claim to such a future stream of income. How much any individual is willing to pay for a bond, hence the market value of that bond, depends critically upon the rate of interest, for the prospective purchaser will wish to earn at least the going rate of interest on the portion of his wealth that he is holding in the form of bonds. Thus, if the rate of interest is 5%, he will be willing to pay up to, but no more than, $100 for a bond that offers an income of $5 per annum in perpetuity. If the rate of interest is 10%, however, no one will be willing to pay more than $50 for the same bond.

It follows then, from the very nature of bonds, that changes in the rate of interest involve changes in their price; a rise in the interest rate means their market value falls, and a fall in the interest rate means it rises. Changes in the rate of interest thus involve capital gains

---

† The distinction between the demand for transactions and precautionary balances, determined chiefly by the level of income, and that for speculative balances, determined by the rate of interest, is often referred to as the distinction between the demand for *active* and *idle* balances. Since all money is at each moment being held by someone, this terminology is not too helpful empirically.

and losses for bond holders. However, these same changes in the rate of interest do not involve any change in the value of money. If we consider the choice between holding money and bonds, it should be clear that (in addition to offering the attraction of an interest income, which money does not always offer) bonds, when the rate of interest is expected to fall, also offer to their owners the possibility of making capital gains. Under such circumstances they become particularly attractive to hold. But when the rate of interest is expected to rise, the situation is quite the opposite, for then it is capital losses that face the bond holder.

Thus Keynes postulated that, when the rate of interest is expected to fall, the demand for money is relatively low, since people hold bonds in anticipation of capital gains; when it is expected to rise, however, the demand for money is greater, as people seek to avoid making capital losses on holding bonds. This is all well and good, but the theory as stated thus far lacks a variable that will tell us when the rate of interest is expected to change, and in what direction. Keynes's solution to this problem was to consider the current level of the rate of interest.

He argued that, at any time, there is a value of the rate of interest that can be regarded as normal, so that when the rate is above this normal level there is a tendency for people to expect it to fall and, when it is below this level, to expect it to rise. In this view, any individual at any particular moment either expects the rate to fall, in which case he anticipates capital gains as well as interest income from holding bonds and will definitely hold bonds, or he expects the rate to rise, in which case he anticipates capital losses on bonds. So long as these expected capital losses are not enough to offset the interest income from bond holding, the individual will continue to keep all his wealth in bonds. However, if the capital losses in question are expected to be large enough to more than offset his interest earnings, the individual will clearly hold nothing but money. There is a third possibility, namely, that expected capital losses just offset his interest earnings so that the overall anticipated yield from bond holding is zero. In the special case where bonds are perpetuities, so that capital value changes are inversely proportional to changes in the rate of interest, this occurs where the expected rate of change in the rate of interest is equal to the current level of the rate of interest; in such circumstances the individual is indifferent as to what proportion of his wealth is held in money.

For an individual with given expectations about the future level of the interest rate, the speculative demand for money is a discontinuous function of its current level. There is a given value of the current rate above which the expected yield on bond holding is positive, below which the yield in question is negative, and at which it is zero. These yields in turn involve (1) a zero demand for money, (2) a demand for money equal to the individual's wealth, and (3) any demand for money between these two extremes. For the aggregate economy, however, it is postulated that, given the normal level of the interest rate, different people have different expectations about its rate of change toward this value. The lower the current rate the more rapidly people will expect it to rise, hence the more individuals will want to hold all their resources in money; by similar reasoning, the higher the rate the smaller the aggregate demand for speculative balances. Provided the money and bond holdings of each individual are insignificant relative to the totals for the economy, and provided there is some diversity of opinion about the expected rate of change of the rate of interest at any moment in time, the aggregate speculative demand-for-money function becomes a smooth and negative function of the current level of the rate of interest.

The simplest form of the total Keynesian demand-for-money function makes transactions and precautionary balances functions of the level of income, and speculative balances a function of the current rate of interest and the level of wealth, the latter variable being included because the argument about the speculative demand for money is cast in terms of the proportion of its total assets the economy will seek to hold in cash. Moreover, these two relationships are thought of as being additive. We obtain, then, as the demand function for money, with W representing real wealth,

$$M_d = [kY + \lambda(r)W]P \qquad (4\text{-}10)$$

The first term within the brackets represents transactions and precautionary balances, and the second term represents speculative balances.† If we confine the analysis to short periods of time over which

† The parentheses around the term r in this equation indicate that λ denotes a functional relationship rather than a linear parameter. The relationship in question is of course to be regarded as a negative one but, as we shall see below, the whole point of Keynes's analysis of the speculative demand for money is to suggest that the relationship between the speculative demand for money and the rate of interest cannot be treated as well approximated by a stable, linear relationship. The fact that the whole expression is multiplied by P, the

the level of wealth does not vary, this variable can simply be ignored and we are left with an equation for the demand for money similar to that used in the model in Chapter 1.

The equation is similar, but not identical, for the parts of Keynes's analysis that are of particular interest for the behavior of the model concern the speculative demand for money and suggest that it cannot be treated as a simple, stable, linear, negative relationship with respect to the rate of interest. Let us look at this more closely. For the individual the choice is to hold his wealth either in money or bonds, depending upon what he expects to happen to the rate of interest; the smoothness of the negative relationship between the demand for money and the rate of interest arises from the fact that different individuals have different expectations about the future rate of change of the rate of interest at given levels of this variable. The lower the rate of interest the more rapidly it will be expected to rise, and the more people will hold money rather than bonds.

It is a short step from this to argue that at some low level of the rate of interest everyone in the economy will expect the rate to rise rapidly enough to make them either unwilling to hold bonds, preferring money instead, or indifferent between bonds and money. At this point the demand for money in the aggregate becomes perfectly elastic with respect to the rate of interest. The latter variable can fall no further, and any increases in the quantity of money will simply be absorbed without any fall in interest rates. This is the doctrine of the *liquidity trap*, which argues that the interest elasticity of the demand for money can, at low levels of the rate of interest, take the value infinity. As we saw in Chapter 2, this hypothesis implies that, when such circumstances arise, monetary policy is quite without effect, fiscal policy being the only means of economic control. It is clearly a doctrine to be compared carefully with the empirical evidence.

The liquidity-trap doctrine, though it is the most startling of the

---

price level, indicates that this theory, like the preceding ones, is a theory of the demand for money in real terms, that, other things being equal, the demand for money is proportional to the price level. Note though the "other things being equal" here include the level of real wealth. A change in the price level can cause this to change if a person holds some of his wealth in instruments denominated in nominal terms. Thus to say that the demand for nominal balances is proportional to the price level is not the same as saying that a change in the price level will lead to a proportional change in the demand for nominal balances. This is true only if everything else is left unaffected by the change in the price level.

implications of Keynes's work on the subject of the demand for money, is not the only one that is important in the context of the model described in Part I of this book. His analysis of the speculative demand for money rests on the proposition that at any moment there is a level of the rate of interest that can be regarded as normal. There is nothing in the analysis to suggest that such a normal level of the rate of interest can be regarded as constant over time. However, the amount of money demanded for speculative purposes in the economy depends on the current level of the rate of interest relative to this normal level. If the latter changes, so will the quantity of money demanded at any particular value of the rate of interest. This model implies, then, that the relationship between the demand for money and the rate of interest will be unstable over time, shifting around as what is regarded as a normal level for the rate of interest changes, so that the effectiveness of monetary policy and fiscal policy alike is impossible to assess on the basis of a model that treats this relationship as a stable one. Again, this is obviously a hypothesis about the demand-for-money function that is well worth investigating.

Keynes's analysis of the demand-for-money function arrives at conclusions completely opposite those of Fisher. The latter implicitly regards the demand for money as being insensitive to the rate of interest and stably related to the volume of transactions (hence of income) in the short run, this relationship changing only slowly over long periods as the institutional framework surrounding market activity changes. Keynes, though perfectly willing to agree about the stability of the transactions demand for money, by following the Cambridge tradition and treating the problem of the demand for money as one of choice-making behavior, found reason to believe that the demand for money in total could be dominated by speculative behavior to such a degree as to make predictions about it based on transactions motives alone totally inadequate—indeed, totally contradictory to the truth in its implications for any model of the macroeconomy.

Friedman and the Modern Quantity Theory

Keynes's work on the demand for money represents a development of one line of the earlier Cambridge theory, inasmuch as it is based on a much closer analysis of the motives that prompt people to hold money than appears in the work of Marshall and Pigou. However, the view that the demand for money should be treated not as a special matter but rather as a particular application of the general theory of demand is never far in the background in the Cambridge tradition, and another line of theorizing often referred to as the *modern quantity theory*, which receives its most comprehensive statement in the work of Milton Friedman (1956), brings this aspect of Marshall and Pigou's work to the forefront and makes the general theory of demand the explicit starting point of the analysis.

Friedman's contribution to monetary theory is precisely to draw attention away from the motives that prompt the holding of money and—taking for granted the fact that people do hold money—to analyze carefully the factors that determine *how much* money people want to hold under various circumstances. He thus treats the analysis of money in exactly the same way an economist would treat that of any durable good were he asked to construct a model of the demand for it, and in doing so formulates a demand function whose form is dictated by the ultimate aim of testing its predictions against empirical evidence.

Friedman begins by postulating that money, like any other asset, yields a flow of services to the person who holds it. Apart from noting that these services derive from the fact that money is a "readily available source of purchasing power," there is no detailed analysis of the motives that are satisfied by them. All that is postulated about these services is that the more money held the less valuable relative to the services of other assets those flowing from money become. This is but a particular application of the general principle of the diminishing marginal rate of substitution between goods in consumption. As with any other application of demand theory to a special case, the bulk of the effort is put into closely analyzing the nature of the budget constraint and picking out the relevant variables to measure the opportunity cost of holding money. That wealth is the appropriate constraint on asset holding, hence on the demand for money, should go without saying, as it should that the rates of return to be earned by holding assets other than money are the relevant opportunity costs in this case. This much is evident from the work of Marshall and Pigou, but what they do not provide is a careful working out of the relevant definition of wealth to be used in analyzing the demand for money on an empirical level, or a precise listing of the relevant alternative rates of return to be considered. It is here that Friedman's contributions lie. Let us take up the wealth concept first.

The role played by the budget constraint in demand theory is to define the maximum amount that can be bought of whatever the good in question is, or, in the case of an asset, the maximum amount of it that can be held. Now if any individual were to free his assets, durable goods, bonds, and the like, he could certainly dispose of all of them and hold money instead. This stock of assets is what we usually refer to as his wealth. However, if the reader will conceive for a moment of a world in which there are no restrictions on what can be bought or sold, he will see that this does not impose a maximum bound on the amount of money an individual can hold. If he has labor income, there will be no reason why he cannot sell a claim to this income stream and devote the proceeds of this sale to money holding as well. When all is said and done, bonds are nothing more than a claim to future interest income, and stocks a claim on the future income from some piece of capital equipment. There is not that much *economic* difference between trade in these assets and trade in future labor income.

This line of argument suggests that the concept of wealth with which we are accustomed to deal in economics should be broadened to include the present value of labor income as well, or, as it has come to be called, human wealth. Analytic precision certainly suggests that this is a sensible course to take, for the foregoing argument considerably generalizes the concept of wealth, making it quite explicit that income from any source can be regarded as a return on wealth, and that wealth is neither more nor less than the present value of an income stream.

However, there are practical arguments which suggest that, as far as empirical analysis is concerned, there is an important distinction to be made between human and nonhuman wealth. The latter can be bought and sold, and there can be substitution almost without limit within this class of wealth. There is, however, no market in human capital in the absence of slavery, hence not much scope for substitution between human and nonhuman capital in the portfolio. There is some scope, though; an individual is always at liberty to sell non-human assets and spend the proceeds on further education to improve his earning power or, conversely, to neglect his education and accumulate nonhuman wealth instead. The possibilities for such substitution between human and nonhuman wealth are limited and in the context of the demand for money, the question arises whether or not non-human wealth alone is a better measure of the constraint upon the holding of it than is total wealth. There is certainly a problem here, and Friedman's solution to it is to postulate that an inclusive definition of wealth should be employed but that, in recognition of the problems raised by the lack of a market in human wealth, perhaps the ratio of human to nonhuman wealth should also be considered a subsidiary variable in the function—the expectation being that, for a given total stock of wealth, the higher its human component the greater the demand for money to compensate for the lack of marketability of human wealth. The question is an empirical one; certain other economists, while following Friedman's basic approach, have preferred a narrower, more conventional definition of wealth but, as we shall see below, nothing of fundamental importance seems to hinge on this matter.

The opportunity cost of holding money is the income to be earned from holding bonds, equity (in the sense of durable goods yielding a service income to their owners as well as corporate stock), and, if one includes human capital in the constraint, the return on it also. The principle of the diminishing marginal rate of substitution between money and other assets ensures that, if the return on any of these other assets rises, the demand for money will fall.

The return on these other assets has two components. First, the interest (or service) income yielded by them must be considered, but so also must the way in which their market prices are expected to vary, for a forgone capital gain (or loss) is every bit as much a part of the opportunity cost of holding money as interest is. As explained earlier, the price of income-earning assets varies inversely with the market rate of interest, so that the expected percentage rate of change of this rate of interest can be used to measure the expected percentage rate of capital gain and loss from holding other assets. The percentage rate of change of the rate of interest is of course opposite in sign to the rate of capital gain (or loss) it is here being used to measure, and it must be subtracted from the rate of interest itself to obtain the expected yield on the asset it is attached to, this yield being what is forgone if money rather than the asset in question is held.†

Though we have talked about the rates of return on various assets as separate variables, it should be obvious that a change in one rate of return will also lead to a change in all the others. If the rate of return on bonds rises, for example, they will become more attractive to hold, so that people will try to exchange other assets such as equities for them, thus bidding up their price and bidding down the price of

---

† This is of course the same variable that underlies the Keynesian speculative demand for money, but this does not make Friedman's views here the same as Keynes's. The essentially Keynesian step is to relate the expected rate of change of the interest rate to its current level, and Friedman does not do this.

equities, continuing to do so until the rates of return on various assets are brought back into an equilibrium relationship.

If the rates of return on various assets move together, we can greatly simplify the demand-for-money function by picking one representative rate and letting it stand for all the others in the function. Which rate fulfills this role best is an empirical matter, but for the moment let us simply call it "the rate of interest" and include it, as well as its rate of change, in the demand function for money, leaving the question of finding its empirical analog until later. If the rate of return on holding money were constant, we could leave matters here, but if the price level can vary, this is not the case. If the price level rises, the real value of money holdings, denominated as they are in nominal terms, falls, and vice versa. Rising or falling price levels provide a return to money holding, which in the former case is negative and in the latter case positive. The expected rate of change of the price level must be interpreted as an expected rate of return to money holding and, other things being equal, the higher the expected rate of return to money holding is the more of it will be held, and the lower it is the less will be held. Thus the expected rate of change of the price level becomes a potentially important variable in the demand-for-money function.

The price level, as well as its rate of change, should be mentioned. Since money is held for the services it provides its owners, and since these services arise from its being a source of purchasing power, it follows that the demand function for money we have been discussing is one that determines the demand for money measured in units of constant purchasing power. It is a demand function for real cash balances and, if we wish to convert it into a demand function for nominal balances, it follows at once that it must be multiplied through by the price level. Thus this model of the demand for money can be written as follows, where M_d is the demand for money in nominal terms, r is the rate of interest, W is wealth, h is the ratio of human to nonhuman wealth, P is the price level, and all time derivatives denote expected rates of change:

$$M_d = f\left(W, r - \frac{1}{r}\frac{dr}{dt}, \frac{1}{P}\frac{dP}{dt}, h\right)P \qquad (4\text{-}11)$$

with the following restrictions being put on the relationships between the variables in question:

$$\frac{\delta M_d}{\delta[r - (1/r)(dr/dt)]} < 0 \qquad (4\text{-}12)$$

(Other things being equal, the higher the yield on other assets the smaller the demand for money)

$$\frac{\delta M_d}{\delta[(1/P)(dP/dt)]} < 0 \qquad (4\text{-}13)$$

(Other things being equal, the higher the rate of change of prices the smaller the demand for money.)

$$\frac{\delta M_d}{\delta P} = f\left(W, r - \frac{1}{r}\frac{dr}{dt}, \frac{1}{P}\frac{dP}{dt}\right) \qquad (4\text{-}14)$$

(Other things being equal, the higher the level of prices the proportionately higher the demand for money.)

$$\frac{\delta M_d}{\delta h} > 0 \qquad (4\text{-}15)$$

(Other things being equal, the higher the ratio of human to non-human wealth the higher the demand for money.) So long as money is a "normal" as opposed to an inferior good, we also have

$$\frac{\delta M_d}{\delta W} > 0 \qquad (4\text{-}16)$$

(Other things being equal, the higher the level of wealth the greater the demand for money.) Thus this is a theory that specifies certain variables as being potentially important determinants of the demand for money and also specifies the sign of the relationship that the demand for money can be expected to bear toward them. It does not, however, say anything about how large or important any of these relationships are, leaving these matters open to empirical investigation.

One cannot say more than this about this approach to the problem of the demand for money without reference to empirical evidence, and this limitation is hardly surprising. One does not expect conventional theory to tell one much about the relative importance of the various factors affecting the demand for other consumer durables, and there is no reason to expect it to tell one more about the demand for money.

In light of the analytic method Friedman adopts, theory has done its job if it states the problem in such a way as to sort out what empirical questions can usefully be asked. Once this has been done, it remains to carry out the empirical work that will enable one to find out whether the relationships between the demand for money and the variables listed above are important ones, and whether or not they are stable over time. Since it is wealth—possibly defined in a novel way—rather than income that appears in this particular function, and since the rate of interest is but one of several other variables listed as being of potential importance, this model, worked out as it is from the first principles of demand theory, suggests that the demand-for-money function used in the model presented in Chapter 1 may be quite a poor approximation of reality. The answers to the empirical questions posed by this approach, then, are clearly worth having.

5

Further Developments in the Keynesian Approach to the Theory of the Demand for Money

In the preceding chapter we dealt with theories of the demand for money that were, on the whole, designed with macroeconomic application in mind. They were either explicitly macroeconomic in their formulation, as was Fisher's work, or, using Friedman's approach, discussed the problem in terms of the behavior of a typical individual, implicitly assuming that what is true for such an individual is also true of the aggregate economy. Not all theories of the demand for money are like this. Recent work extending the Keynesian analysis of transactions, precautionary, and speculative motives for holding money yields implications for individual behavior that are not so readily applied to the aggregate economy by way of simple analogy. Nevertheless, this work draws our attention to certain factors involved in the decision to hold money, which we might otherwise have overlooked; for this reason alone it is worth discussing.

The Transactions Motive

Modern theoretical work on the transactions demand for money, due to both Baumol (1952) and Tobin (1956), seeks to put the analysis on a more rigorous footing and to draw more precise implications about the variables that determine it than Keynes's analysis did. If one wishes to obtain precise conclusions from a model, he must usually make precise assumptions, and those that Baumol makes are as follows.† He analyzes the behavior of an individual transactor, be it a firm or a household, and he assumes that it receives an income payment once per time period, say, per month.‡ However, the transactor must spread out his purchases over time. For the sake of simplicity in the analysis it is assumed that the whole of his receipts are spent at a constant rate over the period. Thus at every moment, except the final instant at the end of the month when the last item of expenditure is made, the transactor finds himself holding some assets, the as yet unspent portion of his income. His problem is how to hold these assets, given that there exist interest-yielding bonds which can be owned as well as cash, and given that there is a fixed cost involved in exchanging bonds for cash.

Clearly he will try to arrange things so that he minimizes his costs over the period. This problem can be solved in the following way. Let T be the real value of the transactor's income, which is also equal to the real value of the volume of transactions he carries out, r the rate of interest per period, which is assumed constant over the period, b the real cost of turning bonds into cash (what Baumol calls the "brokerage fee"), and K the real value of bonds turned into cash every time such a transfer takes place.

The costs incurred by the transactor have two components. First, every time he sells bonds he must pay a brokerage fee and, since he spends all his income and sells bonds in equal lots of size K, the out-

---

† Baumol and Tobin worked independently on this problem, coming to very similar conclusions about it. Of the two, Baumol took a slightly simpler approach to the problem, and it is his analysis that is followed here. A geometric exposition of the model can be found in Johnson (1963).

‡ The actual time period involved is of little importance, for it follows from the analysis presented below that the level of cash balances demanded for a given level of income per annum is independent of the frequency of payment. See footnote on p. 77.

lay in brokerage fees is equal to $b(T/K)$. At the same time, if money is held instead of bonds, interest is forgone, and this too must obviously be treated as a cost. Since expenditure is a constant flow, the transactor's average money holding over the period is $K/2$, that is, half the amount of his receipts from a sale of bonds. This multiplied by the rate of interest per period gives the opportunity cost of holding money.

The total cost of making transactions, where γ is the cost, can then be written

$$\gamma = b\frac{T}{K} + r\frac{K}{2} \tag{5-1}$$

To find the value of K that minimizes this cost we need only take the derivative of Equation (5–1), with respect to K, set it equal to zero, and solve for K. This gives

$$\frac{\delta\gamma}{\delta K} = \frac{-bT}{K^2} + \frac{r}{2} = 0 \tag{5-2}$$

so that

$$K = \sqrt{\frac{2bT}{r}} \tag{5-3}$$

Since, as noted above, money holdings over the period have an average value of $K/2$, the demand-for-money equation that emerges from this analysis is

$$\frac{M_d}{P} = \frac{K}{2} = \frac{1}{2}\sqrt{\frac{2bT}{r}} \tag{5-4}$$

That is, the demand for transactions balances measured in real terms is proportional to the square root of the volume of transactions and inversely proportional to the square root of the rate of interest.† This can be rewritten as

† Some readers may note that this is but a particular application of a well-known general approach to the problem of inventory management. It should be noted that it follows from Equation (5-4) that a lengthening of the income period, which involves an increase in T for a given level of annual income, will involve an equiproportional increase in r, leaving the demand for money unchanged. The reader may also note that, though Equation (5-4) looks like a continuous function, there is in fact a problem of interpretation here. It is de-

$$M_d = \frac{1}{2}\sqrt{\frac{2bT}{r}}\,P = \alpha b^{0.5} T^{0.5} r^{-0.5} \tag{5-5}$$

where
$$\alpha \equiv \frac{1}{2}\sqrt{2}$$

The reader will note that, in deriving this "square-root rule," nothing explicit was said about the utility of holding money for transactions purposes, or about trading off such utility against interest income. One of the strong attractions of Baumol's approach to the demand for money is that it does not appear to find such notions necessary. All that is needed is that money be the means of exchange in the economy and that there be a cost involved in transforming interest-earning assets into money, that there be a brokerage fee. If one substitutes zero for b in Equation (5-4), the expression will clearly reduce to zero, telling us that, if no cost were involved in selling bonds, there would be no demand for money, even in an economy in which it is the only means of exchange. Without the brokerage fee it would pay to synchronize bond sales perfectly with purchases of goods, so that money would not be held except at the instant at which it passes through the hands of the person selling bonds and buying goods.

The brokerage fee is then the vital variable, and it is important to interpret it carefully. To think of its analog in the real world as being literally a fee charged by a bond dealer for selling assets for a client is misleading, for this puts too narrow an interpretation upon what it represents. The role it plays in the model is that of any cost involved in selling income-earning assets; this could just as well be the time and trouble taken by an individual to sell an asset himself as anything else. To put matters on a very simple level, if it takes time to walk around the corner to a savings bank to obtain cash for a deposit there, one is incurring a brokerage fee in doing so just as much as he would if he were paying someone to sell government bonds for him in an organized securities market.

When the brokerage-fee concept is interpreted in this way, the uneasy feeling the reader may have had that it is somehow unrealistic to treat its value as being independent of the value of the transfer

---

rived from a model that assumes that the size of the average cash withdrawal times the number of withdrawals is exactly equal to T, the volume of transactions. This assumption puts discrete limits on the value K can take. For example, the maximum value K can take is to be equal to T. If we set r equal to zero in Equation (5-4) and solve for K, we would think that a withdrawal of infinite size might result. I am indebted to Alvin Marty for drawing my attention to this problem.

made, rather than being related to its size, should diminish. In any case if we add a component to the brokerage fee that varies with the size of the cash withdrawal, so that each withdrawal involves a cost of $b + cK$, this will simply add a term $cK(T/K) = cT$ to Equation (5-1), hence will have no effect on the optimal size of K.

The brokerage fee is not necessarily the same for all individuals, or constant over time for any one individual. If it arises from the time taken to transform income-earning assets into cash, its value will vary with the value of time to the individual concerned. Time not spent on financial transactions can be spent earning income, and so the wage rate of the individual can be regarded as a determinant of the brokerage fee involved in his financial transactions. The higher the wage rate he could be earning the more it costs him to spend a given amount of time transforming income-earning assets into cash. This is a point of some importance, for it suggests that, if this theory of the demand for money is of empirical relevance, we ought to find that the level of wage rates has an influence on the quantity of money demanded in addition to that of the volume of transactions (or of the level of income standing as a proxy for the volume of transactions).†

This discussion of the brokerage fee directs attention to the fact that income payments in the real world are usually made in terms of cash rather than bonds, and that there may reasonably be costs involved in acquiring bonds in exchange for money at the beginning of each period. So long as this cost does not vary with the size of the bond purchase it does not affect anything. Where g is the fixed cost of acquiring bonds in exchange for cash, Equation (5-6) becomes

$$\gamma = b \frac{T}{K} + r \frac{K}{2} + g \tag{5-6}$$

Since g does not vary with the size or frequency of cash withdrawal, the optimal values of these variables are independent of it, except in the case where the cost of acquiring bonds is so high as to persuade the individual to keep all his assets in cash if he is initially paid in cash. Usually, though, even when modified in this way, the model continues to predict that the demand for money will increase in less than

† The relationship between the brokerage fee and the level of wages developed here was not set out by Baumol and Tobin in their original articles. Here we are applying an insight developed by Thomas Saving (1971) in the context of an analysis of the precautionary demand for money. Joel Fried (1973) and Edi Karni (1974), drawing on a suggestion of Barro and Santomero (1972), independently applied the idea to the transactions demand for money.

proportion to the volume of transactions, that there are economies of scale in money holding for the individual.†

This prediction has two potentially important implications for macroeconomics. The first is that, for the aggregate economy, the demand for money depends upon the distribution of income as well as upon its level. If we assume, as we have before, that the volume of transactions conducted in an economy is in a fixed ratio to the level of national income, it will be apparent that, the more a given amount of income is concentrated in a few hands, the lower will be the demand for money for a given level of aggregate income. This is simply because the economies of scale in money holding discussed above accrue to the individual transactor, so that one person carrying out a given volume of transactions will hold less than two people carrying out half that volume each. If the distribution of income varies, so will the demand for money.‡

The second noteworthy implication of there being economies of scale in money holding is that monetary policy may be more powerful than earlier theories have led one to think. With a given distribution of income, any increase or decrease in the supply of money will have a greater effect on the level of income in unemployment situations

---

† The reader should note that in the aggregate it is possible for everyone to receive one income payment per period and spend it continuously. Somebody must be acquiring continuous receipts and making lump-sum expenditures once per period. It is easy to show that, provided there is a brokerage fee for the exchange of cash for bonds, this type of individual's demand for money will also be proportional to the square root of the volume of transactions and inversely proportional to the rate of interest per period. This point is analyzed in Baumol (1952). The reader should also note that to add a variable component to the brokerage fee adds a term in the level of transactions to the resulting demand-for-money function and, as Brunner and Meltzer (1967) have shown, the elasticity of demand for money with respect to the volume of transactions ceases to be a constant 0.5 in this case, but becomes a variable which approaches a lower limit of 0.5 as the volume of transactions becomes small and an upper limit of 1.0 as it becomes large. How large the volume of transactions has to become before the economies of scale in money holding that this model predicts become unimportant is an empirical question, and in any event much effort has been put into seeking empirical evidence of such economies.

‡ This is not to say that the earlier transaction-based models we have considered rule this matter out, for they do not. However, in discussing them above, it has been implicitly assumed that they lead to a demand function for money for any individual that is not only proportional to his income but is also much like that of any other individual. Assumptions such as these permit the distribution of income to be ignored in formulating an aggregate function.

than it would if the demand for money were proportional to the level of income. At a given interest rate, a doubling of the quantity of money in the proportional case requires a doubling of the level of income to absorb it. If the economy abides by the simple square-root rule in its demand for money, a quadrupling of real income will be the result of such a change. At full employment, though, the price level will move in proportion to the money supply, as in other models, since both the nominal value of transactions and the nominal value of the brokerage fee vary in proportion to the price level, producing a proportional relationship between the demand for money and the price level.

The foregoing implications then give us good reason for taking this theory of the demand for money seriously. They suggest that not only may the linear demand-for-money function used in Chapter 1 be a misleading simplification of the truth but also that the specifications for a function that include only the level of income and the rate of interest may not be complete enough to allow it to form part of a model expected to yield accurate predictions about any actual economy. In particular, this modern approach to the transactions demand for money suggests that both the level of wages and the distribution of income are factors whose influence on the demand for money are worth looking into.

The Precautionary Motive

In a Keynesian framework, the transactions demand for money is only one part of the total demand. The precautionary motive is closely associated with it. Transactions-demand analysis deals with a demand for money that arises even when an individual's pattern of income receipts and expenditures is given to him and known with perfect certainty; analysis of the precautionary motive is concerned with the impetus to money holding generated by uncertainty about the timing of cash inflows and outflows. In recent years several economists have developed formal models to deal with issues that arise in this context. The following represents an attempt to present the key features of this analysis in as simple a form as possible.†

---

† The genesis of this line of work in recent literature is to be found in Patinkin (1965, Chapter 5). Much of the subsequent literature is surveyed by Orr (1970), but the reader's attention is also directed to papers by Whalen (1966), Gray and Parkin (1973), and Goldman (1974). Note, however, that the basic work on these matters was that of Edgeworth (1888).

Consider the behavior of an individual whose income matches his expenditure, not on a period-by-period—let us say month-by-month—basis, but only on average over a number of months. In any particular month there may arise an excess or a shortfall of income over expenditure. If there is an excess, it is added to his wealth, but a shortfall must be made good within the month by decreasing his wealth. As in the Baumol model of the transactions demand for money, the individual can hold his wealth in the form of money or in terms of interest-earning bonds. He decides at the beginning of the month how to allocate his wealth holding over the month between bonds and money. In doing so he bears in mind that money can be used to meet any shortfall of income from expenditure without cost but that, if bonds have to be sold during the month to obtain cash, a lump sum brokerage fee whose size is independent of the value of the bonds sold, is incurred.†

Clearly, a key ingredient in his decision must be an estimate of the frequency with which cash shortfalls of particular sizes are likely to occur, and it is assumed that the individual has knowledge of this. Though he does not know in which month shortfalls of any particular size will occur, he does know the proportion of months in which they will occur or, to put the same matter another way, he knows the probability distribution of such shortfalls. Figure 5-1 shows one particular form such a distribution could take. It portrays a normal distribution. The horizontal axis measures the difference between cash inflows and outflows in any month, and the vertical axis measures the proportion of months in which, on average, a discrepancy between expenditure and outlays of a particular size will occur.

Our normal distribution is drawn symmetrically about zero, and the following assumptions are implicit in its shape. First, equality between expenditure and receipts is a more frequent occurrence than any positive or negative discrepancy. Second, the larger the size of a particular discrepancy the less frequently it occurs. Third, an excess of expenditure over receipts of any given size occurs just as frequently as an excess of receipts over expenditure of the same amount; such

---

† This assumption of a lump-sum brokerage fee is made partly to maintain an affinity between this analysis and that of the transactions motive carried out above, but also makes a crucial contribution to the simplicity of the argument set out here. The relationship between the probability distribution of discrepancies between payments and receipts and the demand-for-money function becomes considerably more complex if a component is introduced into the brokerage fee whose size varies with the magnitude of a bond sale. We take this point up again below.

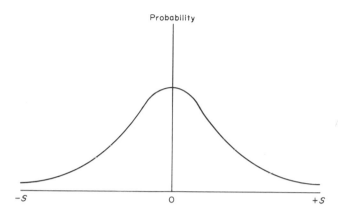

Figure 5-1. The probability distribution of the shortfall (*S*) of receipts from expenditure.

discrepancies cancel out on the average, and our initial assumption of long-run equality between expenditure and receipts is thus satisfied. Nothing crucial hinges upon the precise shape we have assumed for this distribution, although it will become apparent that it is important that at some stage the frequency with which a particular discrepancy arises falls with the size of the discrepancy in question.

It will now be shown that, given our assumptions, a demand-for-money function can be derived directly from the segment of the curve that lies to the right of zero in Figure 5-1.

Consider an individual who enters each month holding an amount of money equal to *M* (in dollars). In those months in which his income falls short of his expenditure by less than *M*, he has no need to sell bonds and incur a brokerage fee, but in all other months he will incur such a fee. The proportion of months in which he incurs a brokerage fee, times the brokerage fee, gives his average monthly outlay for such costs. Where $C(M)$ is the average brokerage-fee outlay associated with holding *M* of precautionary balances, and $p(S > M)$ is the proportion of months in which, or the probability that, the shortfall of income below expenditure will exceed *M*, we can write, where *b* is the brokerage fee,

$$C(M) = p(S > M)b \qquad (5\text{-}7)$$

Now suppose that the individual adds 1 dollar to his money holdings. We now write

$$C(M+1) = p(S > M+1)b \qquad (5\text{-}8)$$

Clearly, the amount that adding 1 dollar to his money holdings saves him in brokerage fees is obtained by subtracting the second expression from the first, and this yields

$$C(M) - C(M+1) = p(M+1 > S > M)b \qquad (5\text{-}9)$$

Or, in words, adding an extra dollar to his money holdings saves an individual, on average per month, the brokerage fee times the proportion of months in which the amount of cash he needs to make good an excess of expenditure over income falls between M and $M+1$.

The saving in brokerage fees we have just discussed is not, however, obtained without cost. An extra dollar held in precautionary balances is a dollar not held in bonds, where it would earn interest. If the rate of interest per period (*not* per annum, but per month) is r (percent), it costs our individual $\$1 \times r = r$ cents, to obtain the savings in brokerage fees we have just discussed. On the assumption that the rate of interest he earns is constant over the month and independent of the number of bonds he holds, the marginal cost of adding to his precautionary balances is constant at r cents per dollar. The individual who is interested in minimizing the costs of dealing with an uncertain pattern of payments and receipts will add cash to his precautionary balances until the saving in brokerage fees obtained by yielding an extra dollar falls to a level at which it just offsets the interest thereby forgone.

Figure 5-2 puts the above reasoning into geometric terms. On the vertical axis we measure both the marginal cost per dollar, in terms of interest forgone, of adding an extra dollar to precautionary balances, and the marginal saving in brokerage fees obtained by so doing. Given a constant rate of interest, the marginal cost curve is simply the horizontal line r, while the curve relating marginal savings in brokerage fees to the amount of cash held is derived from the right-hand segment of the probability distribution drawn in Figure 5-1.

As we have seen, to find the saving obtained by adding the $(M+1)$th dollar to money holdings, we multiply the probability of having a shortfall of receipts from outlays of just $(M+1)$ dollars by the brokerage fee, and similarly for any other value of money holdings. Thus the curve labeled D in Figure 5-2 is simply the right-hand side of the probability distribution depicted in Figure 5-1 with the probability variable on the vertical axis multiplied by the constant

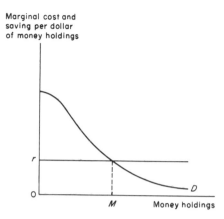

Figure 5-2. The demand curve for precautionary balances.

brokerage fee b. The point at which this curve crosses the horizontal line r obviously gives us the level of precautionary balances at which the marginal benefits obtained in terms of saved brokerage fees just equal the marginal costs incurred. Hence it tells us what quantity of precautionary balances will be held. In short, the curve labeled D is the demand curve for precautionary balances.†

We are now in a position to see what factors this analysis of the precautionary motive suggests we should find influencing the quantity of money demanded. Their effects are depicted in Figure 5-3. First consider the rate of interest. An increase in the rate of interest obviously increases the marginal cost of holding money, shifts the line up from r_1 to r_2, and causes a shift along the demand-for-money function from M_1 to M_2 [panel (a)]. The demand for money also varies with the brokerage fee. If this increases, the marginal savings from holding any given level of precautionary balances will increase in proportion to the change in question, hence the demand-for-money function will shift upward as the brokerage fee increases [panel (b)]. If, as we did earlier, we interpret this fee as referring to the time and trouble involved in exchanging bonds for money, and recognize that the level of real-wage rates tells us about the opportunities forgone in devoting time and trouble to such activity, we will have another argu-

† It should now be clear to the reader why it was remarked above that, although nothing critical hinges upon the normality of the probability distribution portrayed in Figure 5-1, it is important that at some point, as we move to the right, it begins to slope downward.

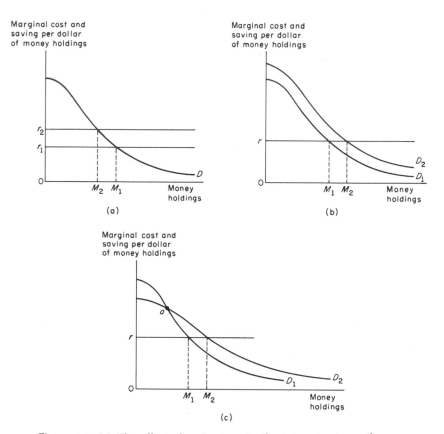

Figure 5-3. (a) The effect of an increase in the interest rate on the pre-cautionary demand for money. (b) The effect of an increase in the brokerage fee on the precautionary demand for money. (c) The effect of an increase in income and expenditure on the precautionary demand for money.

ment suggesting that the real-wage rate should be a variable in the demand-for-money function.

The analyses carried out above all took the level of real income and expenditure as given. In general we can assume that, the higher the overall level of real income and expenditure, the greater the chance of the shortfall of receipts over expenditure exceeding any given value in any period. The precise extent to which this tendency works cannot be deduced unless we are much more specific than we have been about the nature of the processes that cause the patterns of cash inflows and outflows to be uncertain, and about the nature of the interdependence, if any, of the timing of cash inflows and outflows. To carry out such an analysis in any detail is somewhat beyond the technical scope of this book.† However, if an increase in income is, as it usually will be, associated with an increase in the dispersion of the distribution of the discrepancy between payments and receipts depicted in Figure 5-1, it will result in the demand-for-money function pivoting about some point such as *a*, as depicted in Figure 5-3(c). This is because, if the probability of relatively large discrepancies occurring is increased, it must be at the expense of the probability of relatively small discrepancies falling. The sum of the probabilities attached to all possible discrepancies must always, by definition, equal unity.

The implication of this argument about the effect of an increase in the average volume of payments and receipts on the demand-for-money function is straightforward. The lower is rate of interest, and hence the higher are money holdings initially, the greater will be the positive effect on the demand for precautionary balances associated

---

† Consider the following analysis. Suppose the individual's monthly volume of expenditures is a random variable described by a normal distribution, and that his monthly receipts can be characterized by a similar distribution. Then, provided that in any month the values of receipts and expenditures are independent of one another, the mean of the distribution of the difference between expenditures and receipts is simply the difference between the mean of the two separate distributions. Given our assumption that, on average, expenditures and receipts balance, this difference will be zero. The variance of the distribution of expenditures minus receipts is the sum of the variances of the two independent distributions, and its standard deviation is the square root of this variance. Now suppose that the individual's volume of transactions doubles in such a way that, after this doubling, we can treat the new distribution of expenditures as if it were the result of adding together two independent distributions of expenditures with equal means and variances. Make an exactly similar assumption about the way in which the distribution of receipts changes, and then the new distribution of the difference between expenditures and receipts will have a zero mean, and a variance twice that of the original distribution. But this implies that, when the volume of expenditures and receipts doubles in this way, the standard deviation of the distribution will increase in proportion to the square root of 2. Hence we have derived the result that, other things being equal, the level of precautionary balances that will result in a given probability of having to make a cash withdrawal will vary in proportion to the square root of the volume of transactions. This result will hold only if there is strict independence of the distributions of payments and receipts. Any tendency for payments and receipts to be inversely correlated month by month will reduce the extent of such economies of scale in money holding, and a tendency toward a positive correlation between them will accentuate it.

with an increase in income and expenditure. At very high interest rates, above *a* in Figure 5-3(c), the demand for money will actually fall as income and expenditure increase. This rather odd result—for which, it should be added at once, there is no empirical support— begins to vanish from the analysis when a variable component, depending on the size of the cash withdrawal, is added to the brokerage fee. A formal analysis of the reason for this is far beyond the technical scope of this book. Suffice it to say that it arises from the fact that, as the dispersion of the distribution we are discussing increases, the implied increase in the probability of making a large, *hence expensive*, withdrawal increases. The effect of larger withdrawals being more expensive is to give an extra incentive to increase money holding, which is absent from the fixed-brokerage-fee model in which the cost of all withdrawals, regardless of size, is the same.

Finally, it should be noted that, like every other theory of the demand for money we have discussed and shall discuss, this is a theory of the demand for real balances, hence implies that the demand for nominal balances varies in proportion to the price level. If the average price at which each transaction takes place were to double, this would amount to no more than doubling the size of the units in terms of which payments, receipts, and the brokerage fee are measured, and would thus result in a doubling of the nominal quantity of money demanded.

The Speculative Motive

As we saw in the previous chapter, the really novel aspect of Keynes's approach to the demand for money lay not so much in his treatment of the transactions and precautionary motives for holding cash but in his analysis of the speculative motive.

It is hardly surprising then that this branch of his thought has also been worked on recently. As we shall now see, it has been considerably refined in the process.

The speculative motive for holding money arises because, unlike other financial assets, the capital value of money does not change with changes in the interest rate, and because there is uncertainty about the manner in which the interest rate will change in the future. Keynes's solution to such problems was to posit that, as far as the choice between holding bonds and money is concerned, each individual acts as if he is certain about what is going to happen to the interest rate, and hence holds either bonds or money depending upon his expectations. It was only by suggesting that different people, at any time, have different expectations about the rate of change of the interest rate that, in the aggregate, Keynes achieved a smooth relationship between the speculative demand for money and the rate of interest.

Modern work on this problem, due chiefly to Tobin (1958), has concentrated on producing a more sophisticated analysis of the behavior of the individual.† Such an endeavor as this is obviously necessary, since even quite casual observation shows that one does not find individual wealth holders owning either nothing but money or nothing but bonds, or "nothing but" any other single asset one could name. Rather, people hold diversified portfolios, a mixture of assets. Such behavior cannot be explained by a theory that posits that people behave as if they were certain about the future. If they were, they would hold only the asset they expect to yield the highest return. The holding of diversified portfolios needs explaining. The theory now described—though it is here confined to dealing with the problem of diversification between money and bonds—is one that is capable of quite general application to this problem.

The key to the analysis is a relatively simple proposition about people's tastes: They treat wealth as a "good," but they treat risk as a "bad," something that reduces the satisfaction derived from wealth. To give a concrete example, it is postulated that people prefer, say, $100 offered to them with certainty to a fifty-fifty chance of receiving either $50 or $150. In both cases the expected gain is $100, in the first case because the sum is guaranteed and in the second because, if the offer is accepted many times, on half the occasions $50 will be forthcoming and on the other half $150, making $100 on average. However, in the second case there is a risk attached to the outcome, and this is thought of as reducing the desirability of this alternative. If the

---

† The analysis that follows is not a straight exposition of Tobin's article. In particular it differs in making utility a function of expected wealth and risk rather than a function of the expected rate of return on a portfolio and risk. The latter procedure involves an assumption that the composition of a portfolio is independent of its size, that the wealth elasticity of the demand for money and bonds is unity; this assumption rules out the interesting possibility of a perverse relationship between the demand for money and the rate of interest dealt with below. Tobin's original paper is not altogether clear on this matter, and I am indebted to Peter Diamond for first drawing my attention to some of the problems involved.

risk were larger—say the possible sums were $25 and $175—the alternative would be even less desirable.†

Now let us see how this quite simple and appealing notion can be applied to the problem of the speculative demand for money. Consider an individual who receives his income once per period and who saves. He must have some form of holding his savings between periods, so let the assets available to him be money and bonds. If we assume the price level to be constant, there is no question of money either earning a return for or imposing any risk on the person who holds it. However, since bonds pay interest and are subject to fluctuations in price, they yield income—albeit an uncertain one. This income has two components: the interest payments accruing to the bond holder, an amount we take as certain, and capital gains and losses which must be predicted. For the sake of simplicity in the analysis that follows we assume that the individual, when he assesses the probabilities of making capital gains and losses on bonds, does so in such a way as to make the expected value of such gains and losses zero, so

† The notion of a trade-off between risk and return in fact follows from the assumption that the marginal utility of wealth falls as wealth increases. Consider the accompanying diagram, where wealth (W) is measured on the horizontal axis and utility (U) is measured cardinally on the vertical axis. $100 with certainty yields a utility of $U(100)$, while a fifty-fifty chance of $150 or $50

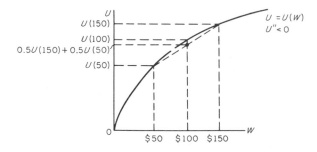

yields a fifty-fifty chance of $U(150)$ or $U(50)$, and the average utility expected here is obviously less than $U(100)$ because $50 in excess of $100 represents less of a gain than $50 subtracted from $100 represents a loss. This is because the marginal utility of wealth is diminishing. Clearly, a similar argument would show that a fifty-fifty chance of $25 or $175 would yield even less utility. This analysis becomes more complex as continuous distributions are attached to potential outcomes of situations but, provided the distributions in question are normal, it is possible to treat utility as a function of expected wealth and the standard deviation of the distribution about this expected value, the latter variable measuring risk.

that the expected value of the yield on holding bonds becomes just equal to the market rate of interest.† However, there is a risk attached to the return to be had from holding bonds, which can be measured by the standard deviation, a common measure of dispersion, of the probability distribution in terms of which the individual describes his expectations about the future price of bonds.‡

Now the problem confronting the individual at the end of a period is to allocate his savings, whose amount it is assumed has already been decided, between bonds and money so as to maximize the utility he expects to derive from them. Holding more bonds increases the expected interest income to be earned on his savings and, since this increases the wealth he expects to have in the next period, it tends to increase his utility. However, it also increases the dispersion of the possible values his wealth will take in the next period. The more bonds in his portfolio whose price can fluctuate, the greater the possible fluctuation in the value of the portfolio.§ Since risk reduces the individual's utility, the introduction of extra bonds into the portfolio involves trading off extra expected wealth in the next period against extra risk. A diagram or two will help to make this clear and will enable us to carry the analysis further.

In Figure 5-4, expected wealth in the next period w is measured on the vertical axis, and risk σ on the horizontal axis. The curves I_0, I_1, and so on are *indifference curves*, whose interpretation is familiar.

† This assumption is not a necessary one. One may have a positive or negative expected value of capital gains and losses without basically altering the analysis. However, to take this approach complicates things, for the slope of the budget constraint in the figures that follow is no longer given by the interest rate in such a case, but rather by the interest rate plus the expected rate of capital gain. Unless one can relate the latter variable to the interest rate, perhaps in the way Keynes did, the relationship between the demand for money and the interest rate produced by this theory becomes obscure.

‡ The use of the standard deviation of this distribution is not arbitrary but is in fact dictated by the utility theory that underlies this model. On this matter the skeptic can consult Tobin (1958).

§ In the model discussed here, holding more bonds means bearing more risk. It is not difficult to think of a model in which it is money that is the risky asset. For example, if the bonds in question are redeemable at a given value in real terms in the next period, and if the price level in the next period is uncertain, it is money holding that involves risk. However, in a model such as this, an individual will still hold a diversified portfolio and the demand for money will still vary with the rate of interest. Matthews (1963) deals with several aspects of this type of problem.

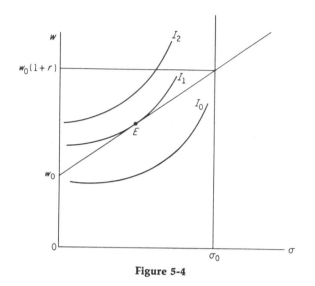

Figure 5-4

Each curve represents a locus of combinations of expected wealth and risk between which the individual is indifferent. Each curve slopes upward to the right as a result of the assumption that expected wealth is a "good," something that adds to utility, and risk is a "bad," something that detracts from it. It follows from this assumption that, if his wealth is increased, the individual will be better off unless risk is also increased to hold him at the same level of satisfaction as before. For the same reason, the indifference curves are to be interpreted as reflecting higher levels of utility as one moves upward and to the left. More wealth with no extra risk attached, or less risk with no compensating decrease in wealth, make the individual better off. The curves are convex downward, because it is posited that the more wealth owned the less some extra wealth will mean to the individual, and hence the smaller the increase in risk he will be willing to bear to increase his expected wealth further.

   The line $w_0 - w_0(1+r)$ is the budget constraint, the line that shows the combinations of risk and expected wealth the individual can actually choose from in arranging his portfolio. If he chooses to hold all his wealth in the form of money, he will earn no return on it, but neither will he face any risk. Hence the budget constraint passes through the point w_0, which measures the amount of wealth he initially begins with and the amount he will end up with if he holds it all in the form of money. Similarly, if he chooses to hold all his wealth in bonds, his expected wealth in this circumstance will be equal to $w_0(1+r)$, where r is the rate of interest and σ_0 is the maximum risk the wealth holder can bear, that which is involved when all his assets are held in the form of bonds. If all bonds are assumed to be the same in terms of the interest they offer and the risk that holding them carries with it, any point along $w_0 - w_0(1+r)$ is available to the wealth holder; he can mix money and bonds in his portfolio, and the more of the latter he holds the proportionately more return he can expect to earn, while the risk he is taking also increases in proportion to the bond content of his portfolio.

Now the wealth holder's problem is to obtain the maximum amount of utility from his portfolio, given the rate of interest and given the riskiness attached to holding bonds. His aim is to reach the highest indifference curve available to him, and this is clearly at the point E where the budget constraint is just tangent to indifference curve I_1. At this point he will be holding a portfolio consisting partly of money and partly of bonds. This analysis then succeeds in explaining asset diversification in portfolios, but its use extends beyond this, for one can use it to derive a relationship between the market rate of interest and the demand for money.

Consider Figure 5-5, which is essentially the same as Figure 5-4. If the market rate of interest is r_1 rather than r_0, and the riskiness of bonds is the same, the slope of the budget constraint obviously will become steeper. Instead of being in equilibrium at E_0 the wealth holder will settle at E_1, which in Figure 5-5 is to the right of, and above, E_0. Thus he will be earning more return and bearing more risk. However, though the rate of interest is different in the two situations, the riskiness of bonds is not, so the conclusion that more risk is being borne implies at once that more bonds are being held at a higher rate of interest. That is to say, the higher the rate of interest the smaller the demand for money. From this analysis it is possible to derive for the individual a speculative demand curve for money that is continuous and downward sloping, unlike the Keynesian approach, which yields a smooth relationship only in the aggregate.

However, the relationship does not *have* to be downward sloping, for its nature depends upon the indifference curves from which it is derived. It is quite possible to draw these so that at a higher rate of interest less risk is taken (that is, more money is held) or indeed so that just the same amount of money is held; these possibilities are shown in Figure 5-6. The nature of the demand-for-money function

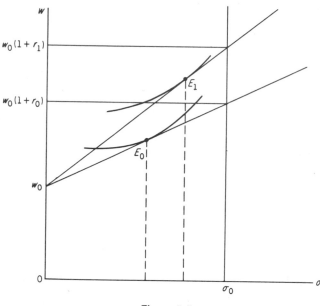

Figure 5-5

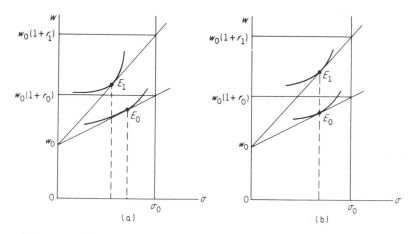

Figure 5-6. (a) An indifference map that yields a higher demand for money at higher rates of interest. (b) An indifference map that yields the same demand for money at different rates of interest.

derived from this analysis depends upon the nature of the indifference map posited as underlying it and becomes an empirical matter rather than one of theory. This should not perturb the reader unduly, for such conclusions often emerge in economics.†

This is no more than a case of the substitution effect and the income effect (it may be better to call it the *wealth effect* here) potentially working in opposite directions. Consider Figure 5-7 which reproduces Figure 5-5. The movement from E_0 to E_1 can be regarded as being partly a movement around an indifference curve and partly a movement to a higher one. The substitution effect $E_0 - E_2$ clearly leads to less money being held at a higher rate of interest, but the wealth effect from $E_2 - E_1$ could go either way. However, so long as an increase in wealth leads people to desire to hold more bonds, the wealth effect of a higher rate of interest will reinforce the substitution effect and lead to more bonds, and hence less money, being held. Since this seems so reasonable a postulate about the nature of the relationship between the level of wealth and the demand for bonds, the possibility of a perverse relationship between the demand for money and the rate of interest seems to be virtually ruled out.

It should be stressed here that we are dealing with the relationship between the demand for money and the rate of interest for an individual who has a given amount of wealth to allocate between money and bonds. This is not necessarily the same as the relationship between the demand for money and the rate of interest when the rate of interest changes, for the simple reason that changes in the rate of interest will leave wealth unaltered only for individuals who were not holding bonds at the time the rate changed. For those who were holding bonds, a rise in the rate would involve a fall in their wealth, and vice versa. So long as the demand for money changes in the same direction as wealth, so long as money has a positive wealth elasticity of demand, these effects will reinforce the already analyzed tendency of the relationship between the demand for money and the rate of interest to be negative.

The effect of changes in the riskiness of bonds on the demand for money should also be discussed. In terms of our diagrams, an increase

† The possibility of a "backward bending" supply curve of labor is a famous example of this and, indeed, if the reader will but substitute income for w on the vertical axis of Figure 5-4, and hours worked for σ on the horizontal axis and interpret the intercept of the budget constraint as being nonlabor income and its slope as being equal to the wage rate, he will find that he has exactly the model that can yield this implication.

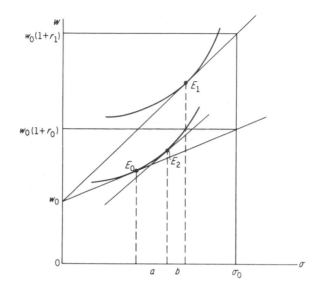

Figure 5-7. The distance a represents a substitution effect, b the wealth effect, and $a+b$ the total effect of the rate of interest being r_1 rather than r_0.

in the riskiness of bonds involves a shift to the right of σ_0, so that the budget constraint becomes more shallow at a given rate of interest. This is shown in Figure 5-8, and the reader will be able to see quite clearly that greater riskiness of bonds has an effect that is in every way equivalent to a lower interest rate, increasing the quantity of money demanded. Similarly, a decrease in the riskiness of bonds will cause the demand for money to decrease. These results are quite plausible. It is interest that makes bonds attractive to hold, and riskiness that detracts from their desirability. A rise in the interest rate and a decrease in risk are alternative ways of making bonds more attractive to hold, and it is hardly surprising that they work in equivalent ways.

We have here, then, a theory of the speculative demand for money by an individual, which suggests that it depends upon the individual's wealth, the rate of interest (which in this theory stands for the expected yield on holding bonds over some period), and the standard deviation of the probability distribution the individual attributes to possible rates of capital gain and loss on bonds—the risk attached to holding them. Though nothing is explicitly said about the price level here, it should be clear that, since the utility function underlying this

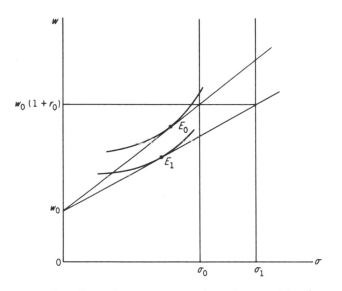

Figure 5-8. The effect of an increase in the riskiness of bonds causes a movement from E_0 to E_1.

analysis makes utility a function of real wealth, it is again a function in which, other things being equal, the demand for money measured in nominal terms is proportional to the price level. [But remember that saying the demand for money is proportional to the price level (other things being equal) is not the same as saying that a change in the price level will necessarily lead to a proportional change in the demand for money. The "other things" may not remain equal. See footnote on p. 66.]

The key characteristic of this theory, as we have presented it, is that it deals with the allocation of wealth between two assets, the return on one being certain and the return on the other being subject to risk. The reader should note that there is nothing about the *zero* rate of return on money that is essential to the results generated. It is its certainty that matters. If money were to bear a positive, but still certain, rate of return r_m, the only difference this would make to the above analysis would be to shift the intercept of the budget constraint with the vertical axis of our diagrams up from w_0 to some point $w_0(1+r_m)$. As we shall see in the next chapter, this is an important point to consider when deciding how to test hypotheses arising from this model.

This is, in any event, a model of individual behavior, and concerns only part of the individual's overall demand for money. We should not claim that it tells us too much about the nature of the aggregate demand-for-money function. However, inasmuch as it is a theory that explains the holding of diversified portfolios by individuals, there can be little doubt that, if speculative motives are important in the aggregate, they are probably better analyzed in terms of a model such as this than in terms of Keynes's approach. The latter does not allow for portfolio diversification. Even so, this approach gets us a little further forward in formulating hypotheses about the nature of the economy's aggregate demand-for-money function. It suggests that some measure of the economy's assessment of the riskiness of assets other than money may be worth including in that function.

Conclusions

As already noted, each of the three approaches to the analysis of the demand for money we have dealt with in this chapter is cast in terms of individual behavior. Moreover, each of them deals with only one aspect of an individual's demand for money. They do not therefore directly yield predictions about the nature of the economy's aggregate demand-for-money function, the relationship upon which this book is focused. Nevertheless, this work is still extremely relevant; it does not tell us directly about the aggregate demand-for-money function, but it gives us several hints about its possible nature. Thus: if economies of scale exist in individual demand functions they may also exist in the aggregate, while distributional effects may be important; if brokerage fees influence individual behavior, and these involve costs measured in terms of time and trouble, it may be that the aggregate demand for money varies with the level of real wages ruling in the economy; and if the riskiness of bonds influences individual behavior, it may be that such a factor is also important in the aggregate. Therefore, quite apart from being interesting pieces of analysis in their own right, these recent extensions of Keynesian theorizing about the nature of the demand-for-money function also raise interesting questions about aggregate behavior that are worthy of empirical investigation.

PART

III

THE EMPIRICAL EVIDENCE

6

Problems of Empirical Testing: The Data and the Identification Problem

Before empirical tests are discussed something should be said about the data used in carrying them out, as well as about the statistical techniques employed. In the foregoing theoretical discussions we talked about money, the rate of interest, wealth, and the like, as if it were quite clear what these words referred to. The reader has no doubt some rough idea of what is meant by each of these terms, an idea that suffices for understanding of the logic of the theories. However, if empirical tests are to be carried out, a precise definition must be given for each term so that data can be gathered and precise empirical hypotheses based on the various models of the demand for money can be formulated.

The Definition of Money

Consider first the problem of finding an empirical definition of money. There is no sharp distinction in the real world between money and other assets, but rather a spectrum of assets, some more like one's rough idea of money than others. Though some theories are fairly explicit on where the line should be drawn in this spectrum of assets, others are not. The theories explicitly based on the transactions motive for holding money emphasize the proposition that a demand for money exists because, unlike other assets, money is a means of exchange. Such theories are theories of the demand for assets that are readily acceptable and transferable in everyday transactions, and the money concept to which they apply is easily definable in the context of the United States economy; there are but two assets that have such a characteristic. These are currency and demand deposits at commercial banks. The sum of these assets available to the public at any time constitutes the relevant measure of the money stock so far as theories of the transactions demand for money are concerned.

For the British economy things are equally clearcut, for only currency and current accounts at commercial banks can be regarded as generally acceptable means of exchange. Matters are not always so simple, however. In Canada, for example, certain classes of deposits at trust companies (institutions somewhat similar to savings and loan associations) are transferable by check, as are certain classes of time deposits at chartered banks; however, in these cases the charges levied for making transfers by check may be sufficiently high as to deter people from using such assets as if they were the equivalent of ordinary checking accounts. It is far from obvious a priori whether or not it is appropriate to treat such assets as means of exchange. Thus it may be clear in some countries which assets constitute a means of exchange, but this is not always the case.

Moreover, not all theories of the demand for money are based on the transactions motive. As a result, even for such economies as those of the United States and Great Britain it is hard to settle on an appropriate definition of money on a priori grounds. Theories of the speculative demand for money totally ignore its characteristic as a means of exchange and emphasize instead the fact that it is an asset whose capital value does not vary with the rate of interest. Currency and demand deposits have this characteristic to be sure, but they are not the only assets that possess it. Time deposits at commercial banks, deposits at mutual savings banks, and savings and loan association shares are, from this point of view, just as much "money" in a United States context as are their equivalents in other economies. Such assets as these yield an interest income to their holders at a rate higher than that borne by demand deposits and currency. The extent to which demand deposits bear interest varies from time to time and place to place, but it would be hard to find a case of their bearing interest at a rate higher than that available on time deposits and such.† Currency—except very occasionally in the past in the case of notes issued by privately owned banks—is an asset that bears no interest. Despite this, individuals hold currency and demand deposits in significant amounts, and the speculative motive for holding money can be of little relevance as far as the demand for "narrow money" is concerned. It is more likely to play a role in determining the demand for such assets as time deposits. Hence its importance can best be tested in the context of the demand for money defined over a broader spectrum of assets than currency and demand deposits.

Theories based on the precautionary motive yield no clearcut guide as how best to define money for empirical purposes. There is no doubt that currency and demand deposits may be held for precautionary reasons. However, it can be argued that the costs of transferring funds from a time deposit to a demand deposit when they are needed to cover an unexpected cash outflow are small relative to those involved in converting, say, savings and loan association shares into a demand deposit. If this argument is correct, it will follow that time deposits can reasonably be included in a definition of money to which the theory of the precautionary demand for money is relevant. At the very least, the existence of such an argument prevents such a possibility from being ruled out a priori.

Theories of the demand for money that rest simply on the proposition that money yields a flow of unspecified services to its owners raise similar problems. Every asset yields services to its owner, and in defining one set of assets as being money and another as not being money, one is really arguing that the services yielded by the various assets in the first category are sufficiently similar to one another to make it possible to treat them as if they were all one asset, and sufficiently different from those yielded by other assets to disqualify the latter from being put in the same category. It is the asset holder's decision, rather than that of the economist studying his behavior, that determines which assets are close substitutes for one another and which are not. The only way to find out what asset holders think is to study their behavior; in the context of this more general approach to the problem of the demand for money, the correct definition of money becomes an empirical matter.

---

† See pp. 110–111 for a discussion of the rate of return on demand deposits.

If an economist wishes to investigate the empirical nature of the demand-for-money function and is convinced before he begins that transactions motives dominate the function, he will, if he is studying the United States, choose to define money as currency in the hands of the public plus demand deposits at commercial banks. However, one of the principal objects of doing empirical work is to discover whether or not transactions motives do indeed dominate the function. One will hardly be able to solve this problem by assuming the answer to it when he designs his test. Thus several definitions of money have been employed in the course of testing theories of the demand for money.

As far as the United States economy is concerned, the bulk of the work carried out has confined the definition of money to currency plus demand deposits at commercial banks, or currency plus demand deposits plus time deposits at commercial banks. There is a good reason for so limiting the definition of money, for in addition to clarifying the theory of the demand for money per se, these empirical tests are supposed to throw light on the scope of economic policy, particularly monetary policy. One wishes, then, to know about the role played in the economy by assets whose volume can be controlled by the monetary authorities, and these assets are currency in circulation and the liabilities of commercial banks. It is thus not unreasonable to concentrate on these assets to the exclusion of others, though of course, had it turned out that a stable demand function for money could not be identified without broadening the money concept beyond these limits, work could not have stopped here. In the event, though, it does not seem to be necessary to extend further the definition of money, for, as we shall see below, stable demand functions can be found utilizing both a definition of money that stops short of time deposits and one that includes these assets. Indeed, we shall also see that there are grounds for arguing that, of these two definitions of money, it is the narrow one that is marginally to be preferred.

Far more work has been done on the demand for money in the United States economy than in any other, but many other countries have been studied with less thoroughness. To discuss the details of the definitions of money used in studies of these other countries would require us to go into a degree of detail about their individual financial systems that would be quite inappropriate in a book such as this. Suffice it to say that, as far as possible, people working on countries other than the United States have tried to utilize definitions of money roughly corresponding to those used in studying United States data, some a little broader in scope and some a little narrower, and that, as with the United States, many results have in fact turned out to be independent of the precise choice of the definition of money.

Measures of Income and Wealth

So much for the appropriate definition of the dependent variable of the demand-for-money function. Let us now turn to the independent variables in the relationship. These fall into three groups. First, there are what we shall call the *scale* variables in the relationship, wealth and income; second, there are the *opportunity cost* variables, the yields on assets other than money, and the yield on money itself, including the expected rate of inflation; finally, there are the *other* variables that particular approaches to the theory of the demand for money suggest may be relevant, the level of wages, the riskiness of bonds, and so on. We deal with the scale variables first of all.

The level of income is often thought of as standing as a proxy for the volume of transactions in the economy, and hence has played an important role in empirical tests of transactions-based theories of the demand for money. It is also important because it is one of the principal arguments in the demand-for-money function utilized in the macroeconomic model presented in Part I. The measurement of this variable presents little problem because, although gross national product and net national product series have been used to measure it, as well as gross domestic product series in some cases, these variables move so closely together over time that no important difference in results is obtained by using one or the other.

The empirical measurement of wealth is not so straightforward. As far as the United States is concerned, data exist that permit the construction of series for various measures of the aggregate level of non-human wealth owned by the private sector of the economy.† Suffi-

---

† There is a problem here as to how much consolidation there should be of the wealth data in producing an aggregate figure. For example, if households own firms, as they do, and one thinks of household wealth as the constraint upon household money holding, and firm wealth as the constraint upon firm money holding, should one, in aggregating the two to obtain the constraint upon the combined money holding of firms and households, ignore the fact that firm wealth is in fact included in household wealth, being the value of the stock households own? Should one simply add the two wealth figures together, or should one remove all elements of double counting from the aggregate wealth of the two sectors? There is no straight theoretical answer to this question, but empirical work by Meltzer (1963) seems to show that the results achieved are not importantly influenced by the degree of such consolidation in the wealth

ciently detailed data for a long enough time span do not exist for other economies, and so the United States is the only economy for which demand-for-money functions including the level of nonhuman wealth have been fitted.

However, as pointed out earlier, Friedman suggested that a more inclusive concept, embodying the value of human capital as well as nonhuman wealth, should be employed when measuring the constraint on the demand for money. To measure such a concept directly presents formidable difficulties. It is fortunate that a fairly straightforward way around such problems has been found. Wealth is the discounted present value of expected future income and, so long as the rate of discount used can be regarded as constant, wealth varies in exactly the same fashion as expected income. If expected income rises by 10%, so will wealth; if it falls, so will wealth.

One is interested in studying the relationship between *variations* in the level of wealth and *variations* in the demand for money and, because this is the case, it is not important whether wealth is measured directly or whether expected income is used as a proxy for this variable. If expected income were a difficult concept to measure, this substitution would not be much help. However, it has turned out, in the case of more than one variable used in empirical economics, that the value it is expected to take in the future can usefully be measured by applying what is interchangeably termed the *error-learning* or *adaptive-expectations* hypothesis to its current and past actual values.

Let us call the variable in question X, and let the subscripts t, $t-1$, and so on, refer to the periods during which its value is actually being observed. Let X^e be the value X is expected to take in the future, and let the subscripts t, $t-1$, and so on, refer to the periods during which the expectation in question is held. It is obvious that we can write the change that takes place between two periods in the value X

---

data used. Thus the simplest approach has been taken, and the practice now is to treat wealth as the consolidated net worth of the private sector, including that sector's ownership of government debt. Meltzer's evidence seems to show that, to treat the government as "owned" by the private sector, hence to add government assets rather than government debt to the assets of the private sector, makes a difference in the results achieved. However, some of Laidler's results tend to contradict this conclusion. To treat government debt as net wealth ignores the possibility that the private sector regards the future tax liabilities inherent in the necessity that the government pay interest on its debt as decreasing its net worth. See Appendix B.

is expected to take, the extent to which expectations adapt between two periods, as $X_t^e - X_{t-1}^e$. The error-learning hypothesis postulates that this change is proportional to the difference between the expectation about the value of X held in the period $t-1$ and the value X actually takes subsequently, that is, to the amount by which the initially held expectation turned out to be in error. Thus with b a positive fraction we can write the error-learning hypothesis as

$$X_t^e - X_{t-1}^e = b(X_t - X_{t-1}^e) \qquad (6\text{-}1)$$

Elementary rearrangement of this expression gives

$$X_t^e = bX_t + (1-b)X_{t-1}^e \qquad (6\text{-}2)$$

and from this, by continuous back-substitution, it follows that

$$X_t^e = bX_t + b(1-b)X_{t-1} + b(1-b)^2 X_{t-2} + \cdots + b(1-b)^n X_{t-n} + \cdots \qquad (6\text{-}3)$$

In short, the error-learning hypothesis implies that the expected future value of a variable can be measured by taking an exponentially weighted average of current and past values of the variable, the very simple assumption underlying this procedure being nothing more than that, in trying to assess the future, people take past experience into account—and take more notice of the recent past than of more distant times.

Whether this is a good procedure to use or not is of course an empirical matter but, as far as measuring expected or *permanent* income (as it will be called from now on) is concerned, an exponentially weighted average of current and past levels of net national product appears to perform well. It is this variable that has been used in empirical work as a proxy for the more inclusive wealth concept suggested by Friedman's theory of the demand for money. The same variable has proved very useful in work on the consumption function and was indeed originally developed from Friedman's (1957) work in that field. As we saw earlier, Friedman treats the demand for money in the same way in which he would treat the demand for any durable good, and it is therefore extremely appropriate that a variable generated by work on the consumption function be used in work on his theory of the demand for money. The latter is, after all, simply an application of his general theory of consumption behavior to the special case of a particular durable good called money.

Measures of the Opportunity Cost of Holding Money

Now let us turn to the problem of measuring the opportunity cost variables that could be included in the demand-for-money function. Consider first the question of choosing an appropriate variable to measure the yield to be earned on holding assets other than money. In practice, the availability of data limits the choice to one or two series, particularly when long time periods are to be studied. Thus, for the United States, though there are several available candidates when only post-World War II data are to be studied, notably for example the yield on savings and loan association shares, the series used for studies on longer periods have usually been either the yield on 20-year corporate bonds or that on 4- to 6-month commercial paper. They are the yields to be earned on instruments having 20 years (or 4-6 months) to run to redemption, yield being defined as the ratio to its current market price of the average income per annum to be earned from holding to maturity the instrument in question. This yield thus includes any change in the price of the asset that must take place to bring its current price into equality with its redemption price.

As it happens, the two series in question move very closely together over time, and for the purposes of testing for the importance of the rate of interest in the demand-for-money function one is probably as good as the other. However, for some matters it is important to know to which of these rates the demand for money is more closely related, and there are reasonable a priori arguments as to why it may be either. On the one hand it is argued that the long rate is better because it is more representative of the average rate of return on capital in the economy at any time, and hence is a better indicator of the general opportunity cost of holding money than the yield on short-run commercial debts. On the other hand, it is argued that the latter instruments, because of their short maturity, are closer substitutes for money than longer bonds, so that the yield on them is particularly relevant among the alternatives that are forgone by holding cash. There is merit in both these arguments, but they ignore the fact that much work has been done of late on the problem of the term structure of interest rates, the interrelationship of yields on assets of varying maturity.

The most satisfactory theory of the term structure appears to be one that rests on the proposition that (with suitable adjustment for risk) expected holding-period yields on assets of various maturities tend to be equalized by the market. The yield expected to be earned over any week, say, by owning 20-year bonds, tends to be brought into equality with that to be earned on instruments of all other maturities. This expected holding-period yield of course includes capital gains and losses made over the period. Now if this is the case—and if the planned holding period of money and bonds is a short one, in the sense that decisions to hold money or bonds do not bind the one who decides to do so irrevocably for long time periods—then expected yields on various assets over a short holding period are the relevant opportunity costs of holding money and, if the aforementioned theory of the term structure is correct, this yield on any one asset will be more or less equal to that on any other.

The yield on 4- to 6-month commercial paper is therefore more likely to be a good measure of short-holding-period yields on assets other than money, and hence of the relevant opportunity cost of holding money, than the yield to maturity on 20-year bonds.† Whether it is or not is an empirical question of course, and in fact both rates of interest have been used in various tests. It should be noted that the foregoing argument about the virtues of using a short rate of interest amounts to saying that there are assets on which the rate of return over the relevant holding period is subject to little uncertainty. This in turn suggests that theories of the speculative demand for money have little scope for application in practice because of the existence of such assets, and that the liquidity trap hypothesis may better be conceived of as dealing with the behavior of long-term relative to short-term interest rates than with the behavior of the rate of return on assets other than money relative to the rate of return on money itself. Nevertheless, the issue raised here is an empirical one. Even a little uncertainty about the holding-period yields on other assets may be enough to give speculative elements an important role in determining the demand for money, particularly broadly defined money.

The rate of return on bonds is not the only relevant opportunity cost variable. We have already mentioned the rate of return on financial intermediaries' liabilities, but it should be noted that Hamburger (1966, 1977) has argued that physical assets might also be good substitutes for money, and hence has used the rate of return on equities as an opportunity cost variable. The role of the inflation rate in influencing the cost of money holding will be discussed below.

† The reader who is interested in pursuing this matter will find a good introduction to term structure theory in Michaelson (1973).

Though much of the theoretical work dealt with in Part II treated money as an asset bearing a zero rate of return, such an assumption is hardly empirically accurate. Time deposits in the United States, and their equivalents in other countries, explicitly bear interest, and variations in the rate of return they yield ought to influence the demand for money defined broadly enough to include them. Though in most modern economies cartel arrangements among the banks—sometimes sanctioned by government regulation—result in demand deposits bearing no explicit interest, this is not universally the case, nor has it always been so. It was only in 1933 that it became illegal for banks in the United States to pay interest on their demand deposits, while we have already noted that in Canada even today there are certain classes of interest-bearing deposits on which checks can be drawn. In any event, if explicit interest is not paid to depositors, banks can still evade cartel arrangements by making indirect payments to their customers. Setting service charges at a level below the cost of operating an account, making loans to depositors at preferential interest rates, giving free advice on business and tax problems, to say nothing of more obvious promotional schemes offering free gifts, are among the methods available to banks for making payments to depositors without explicitly calling those payments interest. Thus it is an error to suppose that even narrowly defined money does not pay a return to those who hold it, and variations in such a return ought to lead to variations in the quantity of money demanded.

Despite the foregoing arguments, the great majority of the empirical studies we deal with below have treated money, whether broadly or narrowly defined, as bearing interest at a zero rate, or at least at an unvarying rate which can therefore be ignored. Some workers, however, have been more careful and have included explicit measures of the own rate of return on money in their studies. A key problem here is how to measure the rate of interest actually paid on demand deposits, and two approaches have been taken to this issue. First, it was assumed, for example by Feige (1964) and Lee (1967), that banks vary the interest rate they pay to their customers only by varying the charges they levy for servicing checking accounts. Thus it is argued that variations in the ratio of the total value of service charges to the volume of demand deposits can be treated as a variable which is inversely correlated with the rate of interest on demand deposits, hence can be used as a proxy for that variable. Barro and Santomero (1972) refined this approach and took a survey of commercial banks for the period 1950–1968 to discover how remitted service charges actually varied with the size of the deposit held and in this way derived a measure of the rate of interest on demand deposits.

An alternative approach is that of Klein (1974) who takes as his starting point the hypothesis that banks manage to avoid completely any cartel arrangements and do in fact pay, albeit by covert means, what he terms a "competitive" rate of return to their customers. Klein calculates the competitive rate of return on demand deposits in the following way. The main cost any institution bears in having a demand deposit outstanding rather than some nonmoney liability is the interest it forgoes on the proportion of its newly acquired assets that must be held in non-interest-bearing reserves against that liability. If demand deposits were truly non-interest-bearing, and no other marginal costs were involved, the profit to be made by having an extra dollar's worth of deposits outstanding would be the interest earned on the nonreserve fraction of that dollar that the bank could invest in interest-earning securities. Thus, if the market rate of interest were 5%, and the reserve ratio to be held against demand deposits 20%, a bank that did not pay any interest on demand deposits could earn a rate of return of 4% on every dollar deposited with it. Klein's basic postulate is that competition forces the bank to pass this marginal profit on to its depositors. Hence, in our simple example, demand deposits would bear interest, covertly paid, at the rate of 4%. Klein's actual computations are more complex than this simple example, because they allow for other implicit costs and subsidies inherent in United States banking regulations, but they follow the broad outlines just set out. He applies a similar procedure to computing the competitive rate of return on time deposits also, for although these bear explicit interest, the rate at which it is paid is also subject to cartel arrangements and regulations. He then computes the own rate of return on narrow money as a weighted average of the zero rate borne by currency and his estimate of the competitive rate on demand deposits. When dealing with broad money, the competitive rate on time deposits is included in a similar average.

The final opportunity cost variable we should discuss is the expected rate of inflation. Here, as with expected (or permanent) income, the adaptive-expectations hypothesis has been widely used. Indeed, an early formulation of this hypothesis was used by Cagan (1956) in order to generate a series for the expected rate of inflation in a study of the demand for money in hyperinflations. Thus the expected inflation rate is most frequently measured as an exponentially weighted average of current and past values of the actual inflation rate, although some workers have experimented with other weighting patterns. Frenkel (1977), however, in his recent study of the Weimar hyperinflation, has argued that foreign exchange is a relevant alternative asset to domestic money. He therefore measured the opportunity cost of holding money by the forward premium in the foreign exchange market. He argues that this premium measures directly the expected rate of inflation. Recent inflationary experiences in the United States and elsewhere have generated much interest in the role expectations play in inflationary processes, and some attempts have been made to measure inflationary expectations directly by using public opinion survey methods. Such direct measures have also on occasion been used in work on the demand for money.

One caveat is in order concerning the role of the expected inflation rate as an opportunity cost variable in the demand-for-money function. Assets other than money, such as 20-year bonds and 4- to 6-month commercial paper, whose rates of return are widely used as opportunity cost variables are, like money, nominal assets whose real value depreciates with inflation. Thus, when inflation is expected, the public is reluctant to hold them unless the rate of return they bear is adjusted upward to compensate for the expected erosion of real capital value brought about by inflation. The higher the expected rate of inflation the greater such an adjustment must be. But this is to argue that variations in the expected rate of inflation will to some degree be reflected in variations in these rates of return. This is a factor that must be borne in mind when assessing the results of any study that treats the expected rate of inflation and one or other interest rate variable as simultaneously influencing the demand for money without taking account of their interdependence.

Other Variables in the Function

Relatively little needs to be said about the other variables that may, according to one or another of the theories discussed in Part II, play a role in the demand-for-money function. The real-wage rate, which theories that put a brokerage fee into the demand-for-money function suggest might be relevant, has been used in two studies of the United States, by Dutton and Gramm (1973) and by Karni (1974). The former used an economywide average real-wage rate variable, while the latter used average hourly earnings. The distribution of income has not been directly incorporated into empirical work on the demand for money as yet, nor has any measure of the riskiness of bonds. However, a series that measures variations in the inflation rate has been developed recently by Klein (1975). Inasmuch as such variations may reduce the predictability of the value of money, Klein's measure can be regarded as capturing fluctuations in the liquidity of money, and he has used it as a variable in an empirical study of the demand for money in the United States (Klein, 1977).

The Availability of Data

As far as the United States economy is concerned, data on most of the variables used are available back to 1900, and in some cases as far back as 1869. This is an important point to bear in mind when assessing the importance of the empirical tests described in the next chapter, for this period encompasses a wide variety of monetary experience. Any theory that performs well for the United States economy over the years since 1900 is one that is capable of explaining the demand for money in many different situations.

Until 1913, the money supply in the United States was determined by the international specie-flow mechanism, for the country was on the gold standard and there was no central bank. To all intents and purposes there was no such thing as monetary policy in the modern sense under the National Banking system. The creation of the Federal Reserve system in 1913 changed this, and the monetary history of the country after this date has been a varied one as the central bank has learned how (or perhaps how not) to carry out monetary policy. The first conscious attempt of the monetary authorities to control the economy was followed almost immediately by the violent but short-lived business downturn of 1920–1921, which in turn was succeeded by the remarkably smooth and virtually noninflationary growth of the 1920s; 1929 saw the beginning of what was probably the worst depression in United States history, a depression that did not really end until the beginning of World War II when a full-employment level of economic activity was finally restored. In contrast, the years between 1946 and 1966 saw a period of growth and stability unparalleled in the country's history, but since 1966 the behavior of the economy has been subject to much more fluctuation, both in output and employment, but also in the inflation rate. Virtually every type of monetary experience short of hyperinflation has been encountered in the last eight decades of United States history.

Usable data for testing hypotheses about the demand for money are available for many more countries than the United States, although

not usually over such long time periods. Data on central European
countries for the post-World War I period can be used to test theories
of the demand for money under conditions of hyperinflation, as can
data drawn from China for the period before 1948. Latin American
countries such as Argentina, Chile, and Brazil provide data for inflationary experiences which, though they stop short of hyperinflation,
nevertheless include periods of far more rapid rates of price increase
than any experienced in the United States. Data are also available for
Canada, most western European countries, and several less developed
countries, and by now have been widely utilized. The importance of
this is not only that the monetary histories of these countries have
differed both from that of the United States and among themselves,
but also that the institutional framework of their monetary sectors
provides us with extra variety. In short, information has been drawn
from so many different institutional frameworks, and from so many
diverse monetary histories, that any body of theory that withstands
confrontation with this body of data can be regarded as having passed
a battery of tests as severe as any that have ever been conducted in
the social sciences.

The Identification Problem

Virtually all the tests dealt with in the next chapter are based on
the use of regression and correlation analysis. This is a well-known
method of fitting functional relationships to data, and there is no
space here to go into any detail about it. However, there is one aspect
of this technique that is particularly relevant to the problem of the
demand for money and ought to be discussed here, namely, the *identification problem*. The quantity of money demanded is not an observable variable; all that can be measured is the quantity of money
supplied, and it is only by assuming equilibrium in the money market
that the latter concept can be used to measure the former. There also
exists a supply-of-money function, and questions must arise as to
whether, in relating the money stock to various variables, one is not
in fact inadvertently measuring this supply function, or the combined
effects of both the demand and supply functions, rather than the
demand alone.

A diagram will be helpful in grasping this problem. In Figure 6-1,
we show the demand for money as a negative function of the rate of
interest, and the supply function as a positive function of the rate of
interest. Let the problem be to measure the relationship between the

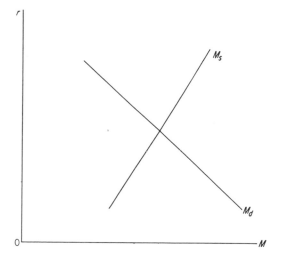

Figure 6-1

demand for money and the rate of interest from observations generated in this market. As can be seen from Figure 6-2, this will be possible only if it is always the supply-of-money function that shifts while the demand function remains stable [panel (a)]. If only the demand function shifts, the supply curve will be what is observed [panel (b)], while if both functions shift, a situation such as that shown in panel (c) will arise and we will obtain a scatter of observations that lie between the demand curve and the supply curve, telling us nothing about either, though we can still use regression analysis to fit a function such as the line FF to them.

The problem is presented here in the two-variable case, but it arises just as much where more than one variable is involved in explaining the demand for money. Before one can take observations of the money supply, relate them to the level of income and the rate of interest, and call the result a demand-for-money function, he must be sure of two matters.

First, he must be sure that the supply function of money shifts independently of the demand-for-money function, that the supply-of-money function contains at least one variable that does not appear in the demand function. It is not hard to establish that this is the case, for the level of reserves made available by the central bank to the commercial banking system figures prominently in any theory of the supply of money and does not appear in any theory of the demand for

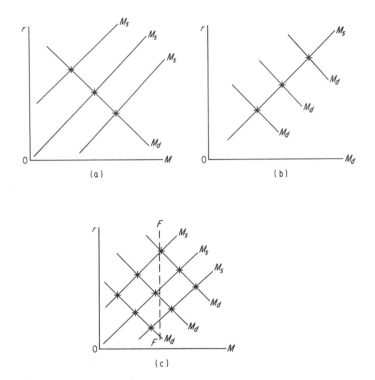

Figure 6-2. (a) Only the supply curve shifts, ensuring that all observations (marked with crosses) lie on the demand curve. (b) Only the demand curve shifts, so that observations outline the supply curve. (c) Both curves shift, yielding a set of observations that, if regression analysis is applied to them, will produce a curve such as FF which is neither a supply function nor a demand function. M is the dependent variable here.

money. There is also ample evidence that this variable shifts around over time, permitting us to be sure that we can obtain observations taken at different points on the demand-for-money function. The second matter of which he must be sure is that such observations lie on the *same* demand-for-money function. It is not sufficient to assume that the supply-of-money function shifts independently of the demand-for-money function; it is necessary to assume that the latter stays put between observations.†

† If the supply of money were totally exogenous, that is to say, dependent in no way on any variable that also determines the demand for money, shifts in

The relationship between the demand for money and the level of income (or wealth) and the rate of interest can be expected to remain stable over time only if these are the only two variables determining the demand for money. If there is some other variable, or variables, that may be important in the demand-for-money function, and if it is omitted from the function fitted, then one is likely to end up with a situation such as that depicted in Figure 6-2(c). The importance of such other variables cannot be ruled out a priori; indeed, anything short of a perfectly stable function will cause a potential problem, so some way of dealing with this matter must be found.

Fortunately, techniques that overcome this difficulty by allowing supply and demand functions to be fitted simultaneously have been used by some economists when studying the money market. Others have used simpler techniques, and to this extent the results they have achieved are suspect. However, as we shall see below, there is quite a bit of evidence that the results for the demand for money are not usually greatly or importantly altered by taking explicit account of the supply side of the market. Hence, in the next chapter, evidence generated by tests that ignore this problem are treated as reliable with one or two exceptions which are explicitly noted.

The identification problem is not of course the only statistical difficulty one encounters doing empirical work on the demand-for-money function. Many other problems arise in interpreting results, but these other problems are not so general as the identification problem and are best dealt with in context as they arise. Let us therefore now go on to discuss the main body of empirical evidence on the nature of the demand-for-money function.

---

the demand function would not prevent us from accurately measuring its parameters. It is interesting to note, vis-à-vis Figure 6–2 (c), that the more the demand-for-money function shifts relative to the supply function the closer the line FF will be to the supply function, and vice versa.

7

The Empirical Evidence on the Demand for Money

The Issues To Be Addressed

The last few chapters have produced various questions worth asking about the demand-for-money function. The most important are:

1. Is the rate of interest an important variable in the function?

2. Is it ever the case that the interest elasticity of demand for money becomes infinite?

3. Is the relationship between the demand for money and the rate of interest stable over time or does it vary with such factors as the riskiness of bonds or the normal rate of interest?

4. In assessing the responsiveness of the demand for money to market rates of interest, is it important to pay attention to variations in the own rate or return on money?

5. Is the interest rate that is relevant for the demand for money a short rate or a long rate?

6. What influence do the expected rate of inflation and uncertainty about the inflation rate exert on the demand for money?

7. Is the demand for money measured in nominal terms proportional to the price level?

8. Should income or wealth, or perhaps both, be included in the demand-for-money function?

9. If wealth is included, should the variable be measured as including or excluding human wealth?

10. Does the level of wage rates have a role in determining the demand for money as theories of the transactions and precautionary demand for money suggest?

11. Are there significant economies of scale in money holding as these same theories of the transactions and precautionary demand for money imply?

12. Is the more appropriate definition of money a narrow or a broad one?

A Summary of the Evidence

As the reader may expect, the answers that can be given to the above questions vary in quality from quite confident to extremely tentative. An endemic difficulty in testing propositions about economic behavior is that it is impossible to hold "other things equal" and investigate only one relationship at a time. The world does not provide data in such a convenient form. In testing a particular relationship it is necessary to assume something about the nature of other relevant relationships. One cannot deal with the relationship between, say, the demand for money and the rate of interest using data generated by an actual economy without also including a variable such as income or wealth in the function fitted to the data, and the outcome of such a test may critically depend upon which of these other variables is chosen and on the particular form of functional relationship chosen for fitting.

It turns out that the answers one obtains for some of the questions posed above are insensitive to this kind or problem. Regardless of the other variables used, and of the form of the functional relationship fitted, the results are the same, and this is true for an encouraging number of issues. Thus the importance of the rate of interest for the demand for money is now established beyond any reasonable doubt, although the evidence is a little less clear that the interest elasticity of demand for money never becomes infinite. The relationship between the demand for money and the rate of interest seems to be stable over time in just about all the economies studied, so that variables such as the riskiness of bonds and the normal interest rate probably play only minor roles in the function. Indeed, we have some direct evidence that seems, on the whole, to point to the irrelevance of the latter variable. At the same time, all the studies that have directly confronted the issue find that variations in the own rate of return on money have a measurable effect on the demand for money. The evidence is not clear-cut on the choice between a long and a short interest rate for inclusion in the demand-for-money function. Some studies point one way, and others another. However, there is evidence that in recent years the rates of return on such close substitutes for money as, for example in the United States, savings and loan association shares, have been of particular importance.

There seems to be little doubt that the expected inflation rate influences the demand for money under conditions of hyperinflation, and also during rapid inflations such as those widely experienced in Latin America. Though most earlier studies could not find a role for the expected inflation rate during the extremely mild inflations that characterized most advanced economies until the mid-1960s, recent work on the United States has taken account of the effects of the higher inflation rates of the last decade and has found the expected inflation rate to be important in the demand-for-money function. As to the role of the price level, a considerable body of evidence gives us little reason to doubt the empirical relevance of the proposition that the demand for nominal balances is proportional to the price level.

Wealth rather than measured income appears to be the superior scale variable for the demand-for-money function. The broader concept of wealth, for which permanent income is the usual proxy variable, has been more widely used than nonhuman wealth; this has been partly because of the lack of data on which to base nonhuman wealth series for most countries, but there is now some evidence that, where series for both variables are available, permanent income performs better than nonhuman wealth. As we shall see, the choice of permanent income as a scale variable for the demand-for-money function raises a whole new set of issues about the role of time lags in the relationship. Only two studies have looked at the role of the level of wages in the demand-for-money function, and both have found it to be of potential importance. There is an increasing body of evidence that, whatever may have been the case for earlier times, the demand-for-money function in advanced economies in the post-World War II period has been characterized by economies of scale.

Finally, we shall see that the evidence on the most appropriate definition of money is equivocal. It seems that, so long as work is confined to long runs of data, observed on an annual average basis, there is really nothing to choose between broad and narrow specifications of the money stock. However, studies of portfolio behavior and of quarter-to-quarter variations in the demand for money both suggest that the narrower definition is to be preferred.

With this brief summary of the evidence in mind, let us now turn to the tests that provided it, beginning with the question of the importance of the rate of interest.

The Role of Interest Rates

Much of the empirical work on the demand-for-money function has taken it for granted that the crucial issue to be investigated is the relationship between the demand for money and the rate of interest. This very Keynesian view of the problem has led economists to design tests that concentrate on this variable and are based on quite simple notions about the role of the other variable or variables in the function, hence making their results rather difficult to accept at face value. In an early study of Great Britain by Brown (1939), and somewhat later ones of the United States by Tobin (1947) and Bronfenbrenner and Mayer (1960), the distinction between active and idle balances was maintained, and it was assumed that only the demand for the latter was responsive to the rate of interest; the problem was to measure the degree of responsiveness involved. In order to obtain a measure of idle balances, the following broad procedure was followed (with details differing among workers). It was assumed that the demand for active balances is proportional to the level of income and that, at some time when the ratio of total money holdings to income is at its lowest observed value, idle balances held are equal to zero. This lowest ratio was then postulated as measuring the parameter m in the equation

$$\frac{M_d}{P} = mY + \lambda(r) \qquad (7\text{-}1)$$

so that, on the assumption that the money market is in equilibrium, idle balances could then be measured at other times as being equal to

$$\frac{M_s}{P} - mY$$

and the demand for them then related to the rate of interest. Differences between these studies in the precise definitions of the variables used, which need not concern us here, did not prevent them from coming to the conclusion that a distinct negative relationship between the demand for idle balances and the rate of interest could be observed. The trouble is of course that the results achieved rest on quite strict assumptions about the nature of the demand-for-money function.

Khusro (1952), in updating Brown's work on Great Britain, found it preferable to treat the ratio of idle balances to liquid assets as varying with the rate of interest, and hence provided the first example of evidence to the effect that some, albeit very narrowly defined, wealth variable plays a role in the demand-for-money function. He also used multiple regression techniques to estimate the value of m, the ratio of active balances to income, rather than using the much cruder method described above, and found that this too improved the explanatory power of his equations which always displayed a significant inverse relationship between idle balances and the interest rate. Bronfenbrenner and Mayer were also troubled by the very strict assumptions about the nature of the demand-for-money function implicit in their initial work, and as an alternative postulated that the demand-for-money function was of the form

$$\frac{M_d}{P} = bYr^\beta \tag{7-2}$$

so that, with equilibrium assumed in the money market, they were able to measure the interest elasticity of the demand for money β by way of the equation

$$\frac{M_s}{PY} = br^\beta \tag{7-3}$$

They fitted this to successive pairs of years, relating the change in the logarithm of the ratio of money holdings to income to the change in the logarithm of the interest rate, and found again that β was generally negative and that this parameter was a better predictor of the direction of change in the demand for money than the hypothesis that this direction of change is a random variable.†

A somewhat similar study by Latané (1954) began with the following demand-for-money function:

$$\frac{M_d}{P} = aY + bYr^{-1} \tag{7-4}$$

from which can be derived

$$\frac{M_d}{PY} = a + b\frac{1}{r} \tag{7-5}$$

Latané found, when using regression analysis, that the parameter b was significantly positive, indicating that the demand for money is negatively related to the rate of interest. He also found that the equation he fitted seemed to have some predictive power over data generated outside the time period to which it was initially fitted.

Now the drawback to all these tests is that they each assume that the demand for money is proportional to the level of income, a postulate that would be challenged by those who regard wealth as a more appropriate variable to include in the function, as well as by those

---

† β is clearly the interest elasticity of demand for money in Equation (7-2), because it follows that

$$\frac{d(M_d/PY)}{dr} = \beta br^{(\beta-1)}$$

so that

$$\frac{d(M_d/PY)}{M_d/PY} = \frac{\beta br^{(\beta-1)}dr}{br^\beta} = \beta\frac{dr}{r}$$

The estimate of β is obtained by using a logarithmic transformation of the variables and fitting the function

$$\log\left(\frac{M_d}{PY}\right) = \log b + \beta(\log r)$$

Note that Bronfenbrenner and Mayer also fitted a straightforward regression of the form

$$\left(\frac{M_d}{P}\right)_t = bY_t^{\beta 0} W_t^{\beta 1} r_t^{\beta 2} \left(\frac{M_d}{P}\right)_{t-1}^{\beta 3}$$

and found the rate of interest an important variable.

who suspect that there may be economies of scale in money holding. Even so, the consistency with which they point to the importance of the rate of interest as a determinant of the demand for money is impressive, and it is fortunate that other work that does not rest upon such strict assumptions confirms this result. By and large, this work is based on regression analysis and, though regression analysis does constrain one to use certain functional forms for the relationships under investigation, the limits are not too severe.

One can, and most recent work on the matter has done so, postulate that the demand-for-money function can be approximated by

$$\frac{M_d}{P} = bX^{\beta_0} r^{\beta_1} \tag{7-6}$$

where X stands either for the level of income Y, the level of non-human wealth W, or the level of permanent income Y^P, and the β's are elasticities, and let a regression equation simultaneously find the values of both elasticities.[†]

Work carried out by Allan Meltzer (1963) fitted such functions for the period 1900–1958, using all three possible substitutes for X, and definitions of money that excluded time deposits at commercial banks (M_1) included them (M_2), and added deposits at mutual savings banks (M_3). Using the rate of interest on 20-year bonds for r, Meltzer found a significant negative relationship between the demand for money, however defined, and the rate of interest, regardless of the other variable included in the function. Though there was some variation in the size of the interest elasticity of the demand for money computed, this variable on the whole seemed to take a value of about −0.7. Moreover, when Meltzer divided his time period up into decades, fitting a separate velocity function to each decade, he found a remarkable similarity in the relationship between the velocity of circulation and the rate of interest for various decades.[‡]

[†] As already noted in the footnote on p. 124, a linear regression performed on the logarithms of the data will find estimates of these elasticities.

[‡] It should be clear that a velocity function is derived from a demand-for-money function by assuming that the demand for money is equal to the supply thereof and dividing both sides by income and inverting the function. Thus, in general, if

$$M_d = f(X,r)P = M_s$$

then

$$\frac{PY}{M_s} = \frac{PY}{f(X,r)P} = V$$

The same economist, in a joint study with Karl Brunner (Brunner and Meltzer, 1963) fitted, for a similar time period, velocity functions derived from demand-for-money functions that used various permutations and combinations of variables, including income, permanent income, and nonhuman wealth. Rather than rely simply on the outcome of regressions, they used a prediction test. A regression equation was fitted to the first 10 years of their data, and its parameters were used to predict the velocity of circulation in the eleventh year; then the second through eleventh years were used to predict the velocity of circulation in the twelfth year, this process being carried out right through their time series. The average errors in prediction made by the various functions were computed, and it was found that the rate of interest played an important role in allowing accurate predictions to be made, while the interest elasticity of demand for money appeared to remain relatively stable regardless of which other variables were included in the function.

Demand functions like Equation (7-6), using successively a short and a long rate of interest and using permanent income as the other variable, were fitted by Laidler (1966b) for the period 1892–1960 and again, regardless of whether the definition of money used included time deposits or excluded them, interest elasticities of demand for money of about −0.7 for the long rate of interest and of about −0.15 for the short rate were found. In this test various subperiods (1892–1916, 1919–1940, and 1946–1960) were also used, and it was found that the relationship between either interest rate and the demand for money was much the same in each period. Similar work was carried out on British data for the period 1900–1965 (Laidler, 1971), using both measured-income and a permanent-income series constructed using the same weights on measured income as had been used in constructing a permanent-income series for the United States. In both cases, interest rate variables proved to have a significant effect on the demand for money, as they did in an earlier study by Kavanagh and Walters (1966) in which a measured-income formulation of the demand-for-money function was tested against data drawn from the years 1877–1961. Studies by Macesich (1970), Clark (1973), and Clinton (1973) for Canada, Teigen (1971) for Norway, Leponiemi (1966) for Finland, and Niehans and Schelbert-Syfrig (1967) for Switzerland —this list is far from exhaustive—all confirm the importance of one interest rate variable or another to the demand-for-money function for these countries.†

† A tabular summary of results obtained by various studies of 13 countries, excluding the United States, is given by Fase and Kure (1975). Also, Adekunle

Of the many studies that have been carried out, we are aware of only three that have failed to find a significant negative relationship between the rate of interest and the demand for money. Thus Laidler and Parkin (1970), studying the demand for money in Great Britain with quarterly data for the period 1955–1967, found that it did not respond systematically to the treasury bill rate. However, the Bank of England (1970), in a study of almost the same period, found no difficulty in discovering evidence of the importance of other interest rate variables in the function; consideration of the rather special role treasury bills played in the British financial system at that time (a description of which need not detain us here) suggests that Laidler and Parkin's choice of variable was inappropriate. Gray, Ward, and Zis (1976) treated the Group of Ten major industrial countries as if they were a single economy and, in fitting a demand-for-money function to data generated by them, found a negative coefficient for an interest rate variable. However, the coefficient could not be estimated precisely enough for them to conclude firmly that it was in fact different from zero; thus their results were indecisive on the matter of the role of the rate of interest in the demand-for-money function rather than definitely suggesting that the variable is not important.

Friedman's (1959) work, for the period 1869–1957, presents more subtle problems. He reasoned that, since by far the greater part of variations in the rate of interest take place within the business cycle, a demand-for-money function fitted to data that abstract from the cycle, if it is used to predict cyclical fluctuations in the demand for money, should yield errors in prediction related to the rate of interest. He therefore took data on the average values of the variables concerned over each business cycle. The variables used were money defined to include time deposits and permanent income, and to them was fitted a log linear regression whose parameters were then used to predict annual variations in the velocity of circulation. He found no close relationship between the errors of prediction and the rate of interest.

Though Friedman was by no means willing to conclude that this evidence ruled out the rate of interest as an important determinant of the demand for money, the results in question certainly raised grave doubts about the matter, and it is fortunate that a refutation of it was forthcoming. Friedman's test is reliable only if the abstracting from

_____

(1968) fitted demand-for-money functions to data for several less developed economies. The importance of some interest rate variable to the demand for money is amply confirmed by all this evidence.

the business cycle that underlies it totally frees the data from the influence of any relationship between the demand for money and the rate of interest. As it happens, for the United States there had been a slight downward trend in interest rates over the period involved and, by omitting the interest rate from his cycle average regression, Friedman caused that part of the variation in the demand for money that was the result of this downward trend in the interest rate wrongly to be attributed to variation in the level of permanent income. Thus he measured the relationship between the demand for money and permanent income erroneously, so that his annual predictions based upon it were not reliable. When a test similar to Friedman's was carried out by Laidler (1966b), the rate of interest was included in the cycle average regression, and this inclusion was found to increase the predictive power of the function for annual data, thus confirming the importance of the rate of interest as a determinant of the demand for money.[†] Moreover, in subsequent, more orthodox work, Friedman (1966) himself found the interest rate to be an important variable in the function.

Now all these tests have one fault in common, and that is that they ignore the identification problem. It cannot be taken for granted that this is unimportant and, fortunately, Brunner and Meltzer (1964) and Teigen (1964) performed studies of United States data that took particular account of this difficulty, simultaneously fitting supply and demand functions for money. The demand function Brunner and Meltzer used in their study was one that used nonhuman wealth and the long rate of interest and, even with explicit account being taken of the supply-of-money function, they found that the interest elasticity of the demand for money appeared to be close to -0.7. The wealth elasticity they obtained (about 1.0) was also similar to Meltzer's single-equation estimate. Teigen, using the level of income and a short rate of interest and the lagged money stock, as well as a slightly different specification of the supply function, found an interest elasticity of demand for money of about -0.15.[‡] As the reader will note, the

---

[†] It was not possible to obtain interest data for Friedman's entire period, so that the data used began in 1892.

[‡] Teigen's study spans the years 1924–1941 (annual data) and 1947–1959 (quarterly data). The introduction of the lagged money stock was meant to take account of slowness on the part of the public to adjust their cash holdings to equilibrium levels, but see below for an alternative interpretation. It should be noted that, because the short interest rate varies more than the long, the computed interest elasticity of demand for money using the former is bound to be smaller.

results cited here are the same as those obtained with similar interest rates in studies that did not take account of the identification problem. Frowen and Arestis (1976) carried out a study of the supply and demand functions for money in West Germany and reported that their estimates of the parameters of the demand-for-money function were relatively insensitive to the extent to which they took explicit account of the identification problem in obtaining them. This evidence suggests that, as far as estimating the demand-for-money function is concerned, the identification problem is not usually a serious one, though we note some exceptions to this general proposition below. The studies discussed so far ignored the existence of an own rate of return on money in investigating the role of the interest rate in the demand-for-money function, but the introduction of this refinement into the analysis in no way undermines the results so far reported. Thus for the years 1951–1964, Lee (1967) used data on the interest differentials between demand deposits and various other assets, including time deposits at commercial banks and savings and loan association shares, to explain the demand for narrow money. With a broader definition of money, he employed the interest differential between time deposits and various other assets and, with permanent income as the other variable in all his tests, he obtained significant results with virtually every interest rate he tried, being particularly successful with that on savings and loan association shares. Unlike Hamburger (1966), however, he did not find the yield on corporate equities a potentially important determinant of the demand for money, although in subsequent work (Lee, 1969), he did find a role for this variable.

More recently, Klein (1974a,b) used his estimates of the competitive rate of return on money described in the preceding chapter in somewhat similar exercises, although for a much longer time period (1880–1970) than Lee. Instead of simply entering the interest differential between money and other assets in his equations, he entered the two rates of return separately and in finding that they took coefficients of opposite signs but similar orders of magnitude was able to confirm, rather than take for granted, the appropriateness of using the interest differential as a single variable. Klein's results are also notable in that they suggest that studies that ignore the own rate of return on money underestimate the sensitivity of the demand for money to the opportunity cost of holding it. When market interest rates rise, so does the own rate of return on money, so that the interest differential between money and other assets changes less than the value of market interest

rates. The observed change in the demand for money under such circumstances should, according to Klein's results, be attributed to this
relatively smaller change in interest differentials rather than the relatively larger change in the overall levels of interest rates. In this
respect Klein's results supplement those of Barro and Santomero
(1972), who reached a similar conclusion by including their measure
of the own rate of return on demand deposits in an equation fitted to
19 annual observations on the demand for money of the United States
household sector.

In short then, whether one thinks of the demand-for-money function as being constrained by income, wealth, or expected income,
whether one defines money to include time deposits or exclude them,
whether one ignores the identification problem or deals with it,
whether one uses a short rate of interest, a long one, or the return on
financial intermediaries' liabilities, or whether one ignores the own
rate of return on money or takes explicit account of it, there is an
overwhelming body of evidence in favor of the proposition that the
demand for money is negatively related to the rate of interest. Of all
the issues in monetary economics, this is the one that appears to have
been settled most decisively.

The Liquidity Trap

This hypothesis states that, at low levels of the rate of interest, the
demand for money becomes perfectly elastic with respect to that variable. It is not possible to fit directly by regression analysis a function
that has a negative slope over part of its range and no slope at all over
another part, so less direct tests must be used. They are not hard to
devise. If the liquidity-trap hypothesis is true, it must be the case that
the interest elasticity of demand for money becomes greater as the
rate of interest falls, since this is the only way it can pass from a finite
to an infinite value. There appears to be little evidence that this is in
fact the case. As mentioned above, Bronfenbrenner and Mayer (1960)
investigated the interest elasticity of M/PY with respect to the interest
rate for successive pairs of annual observations. Over the period they
dealt with (1914–1957) they noted no tendency for the interest elasticities they measured to be higher at low rates of interest. A somewhat similar test was carried out by Laidler (1966b). The time
period (1892–1960) was divided between the years when the rate of
interest was above its average value for the period and those when it
was below it. Such a division was made both for the long rate of inter-

est and the short rate, and regressions of the money stock on the level of permanent income and the interest rate were performed for these two sets of data separately. Definitions of money including and excluding time deposits were employed, and hardly any tendency was discovered for the interest elasticity of demand for money to be higher for low-interest observations than for high-interest ones;[†] nor was there any evidence that the function was any less stable at low rates of interest.

A more direct approach to the question was taken by Pifer (1969). He argued that to fit a log linear function to the relationship between the demand for money and the interest rate was to take it for granted that the minimum conceivable value for the interest rate is zero, because such a constant elasticity demand curve is asymptotic to the horizontal axis. He then noted that an equation that has the form of Equation (7-6) is simply a special case of

$$\frac{M}{P} = bX^{\beta_0} [r - r(\text{minimum})]^{\beta_1} \qquad (7\text{-}7)$$

where r(minimum) is set equal to zero. The relationship between the demand for money and the rate of interest implicit in such a relationship is asymptotic to r(minimum). He then substituted a series of values for this variable into an equation like Equation (7-7), starting at zero and stopping just short of the lowest value actually observed for r. He argued that, if an equation with a positive value for r(minimum) fitted his data significantly better than the equation that set that variable at zero, it would be evidence in favor of the liquidity-trap hypothesis. Pifer applied this test, and a variation on it in which the interest rate rather than the quantity of money was treated as a dependent variable, to United States data for the period 1900–1958 and found no evidence to suggest that there is any well-defined floor above zero for the value of the interest rate.

Kostas and Khouja (1969), using a method somewhat similar to that of Pifer, again on United States data, found some evidence that a long interest rate can take a minimum value above zero, but not a short rate, this phenomenon being important in the late 1940s, however, rather than the 1930s. Their estimation techniques have subsequently been criticized by Kliman and Oksanen (1973) and, since the late

[†] One regression, using the first differences of the data, a narrow definition of money and a long rate of interest, betrayed a tendency in this direction.

1940s was precisely the period in which United States policy was geared to maintaining the rate of interest on government bonds constant by varying the money supply, there must be some suspicion that Kostas and Khouja discovered a perfectly elastic *supply*-of-money function rather than a perfectly elastic demand function for those years, that for once the identification problem was important. Eisner (1971) and Spitzer (1976), both of whom reworked Pifer's tests with more sophisticated econometric techniques and found evidence of a minimum value for the long interest rate, explicitly expressed concern at the absence of any attempt to confront this issue in their own work. It should be noted that the liquidity-trap hypothesis arises when it is postulated that a "normal" value for the interest rate plays a role in the demand-for-money function. Starleaf and Reimer (1967) computed such a variable as a geometrically weighted average of present and past values of the actual rate, took the difference between this variable and the current rate, and related the demand for money to this very Keynesian variable. They found virtually no evidence of its importance as far as the United States was concerned. Robert Crouch (1971) examined the behavior of the interest rate over time in the United States. He found no evidence that it tended systematically to return to some normal value and no evidence that any kind of average of its past values was a better predictor of its future value than was its current value. Such evidence as this goes strongly against the very basis of the theory of the speculative demand for money upon which the liquidity-trap hypothesis is based, but it is worth noting that, in their elaborate study of the Canadian monetary sector, Courchene and Kelly (1971) found evidence consistent with a "normal" interest rate variable playing a role in asset demand functions, though not to the extent of generating a liquidity trap.

Thus the evidence on the liquidity trap is not quite clearcut. On the whole, the evidence goes against the hypothesis, but the results of Kostas and Khouja, Eisner, and Spitzer are, on the face of things, in its favor. These results, however, all depend on the use of a long interest rate. There is no sign of a trap when short rates are used, and this suggests that these workers may be dealing with a phenomenon associated with the term structure of interest rates rather than the demand for money. More likely, the fact that long rates were at a minimum in the late 1940s, when monetary policy was geared to keeping such rates low and stable, rather than in the 1930s when the economy was deeply depressed, points to the possibility that the behavior of the money-supply function, rather than the demand-for-money function may underlie them. Until these conjectures are investigated explicitly though, the conclusion to which we subscribe, that the liquidity-trap hypothesis is of no empirical significance, must rest on an uncomfortably high degree of personal judgment.

Stability of the Interest Rate–Demand-for-Money Relationship

The liquidity-trap hypothesis is, as we saw earlier, closely related to the proposition that the relationship between the demand for money and the rate of interest can be expected to be unstable over time. In fact, this relationship seems to be remarkably well determined. If we consider the United States over the period 1892–1960, the work of Laidler (1966b) shows that the elasticity of demand for money M_2, with respect to the short rate of interest, appears to have varied between roughly −0.12 and −0.15 and, with respect to the long rate of interest, between −0.2 and −0.6. (If M_1 is used instead, the relevant elasticities are −0.17 to −0.20 and −0.5 to −0.8, respectively.) Now it must be admitted that, particularly, as far as the short rate of interest is concerned, these variations seem small and, when Khan (1974) applied formal econometric tests designed to discover the presence of a structural change in the demand-for-money function over a similar period, he found no sign of any such change. The order of magnitude of the interest elasticity estimates found by Laidler (1971) for Great Britain over the period 1900–1965 seem to be similar to those implied by United States data and again show little variation between subperiods.

Teigen (1964) fitted his supply and demand functions separately for both pre- and post-World War II data. Though the earlier period is dominated by the 1930s when the economy was severely depressed, interest rates were remarkably low, and financial markets were extremely unstable, Teigen found no important difference between the two periods in the interest elasticity of the demand for money. Meltzer's (1963) procedure of fitting velocity functions decade by decade revealed a slightly lower interest elasticity of the demand for money in the 1930s than at other times, while Brunner and Meltzer's prediction test produced surprising results. They excluded the years 1941–1950, from their data because of the interest-rate-pegging money supply policy, mentioned earlier, pursued in those years, and still found that regressions weighted heavily with observations taken from the 1930s produced a function that was able to predict the velocity of circulation in the 1950s with no marked falling off in accuracy relative to other predictions they made for other times. Similarly, Laidler's variation on Friedman's test, which employed cycle average data to generate a demand-for-money function which was then used to predict annual variations in money holding, showed no tendency to be less accurate in its predictions for the 1930s than for other times.

This evidence seems to show that instability in the relationship between the demand for money and the rate of interest has never been a factor of particular importance as far as the economic history of either the United States or Great Britain in the present century is concerned.† This evidence, like that on the closely related liquidity-trap hypothesis, comes from studies using a variety of data and techniques. Teigen and Bronfenbrenner and Mayer obtained their results using a short rate of interest and a narrow definition of money, Brunner and Meltzer used both broad and narrow money concepts and a long rate of interest, while Laidler's work involved both money definitions and both interest rates. Functions constrained by wealth, income, and expected income were used in these tests, and the conclusions seem invariant with respect to the many possible permutations and combinations of data involved. Like the conclusion that the rate of interest is an important determinant of the demand for money, the conclusion that the instability hypothesis and related doctrines are of no apparent empirical relevance does not seem to depend in any way on a particular formulation of the demand-for-money function.

The Choice of Interest Rate

The results on the role of an interest rate variable in the demand-for-money function are clear enough then. Such a variable ought to be included in the relationship; there is little reason to suppose that a liquidity trap exists, and no reason to suppose that there is any inherent instability in the relationship between the demand for money and the interest rate. Which interest rate, however? A short rate or a long rate, or the rate of return on some financial asset such as, for example, a savings and loan association share that may be regarded as a close substitute for money? As we have already seen, some studies have used one, and others another, of these alternatives, and for many

---

† The reader should note that, according to an as yet unpublished work by Hamburger (1977), the apparent instability of the demand-for-money function in the FMP quarterly econometric model of the United States since 1974 is a result of the particular opportunity cost variables entered in that function being inappropriately chosen.

purposes nothing seems to hinge on the choice. Indeed, for long runs of United States data, or British data, there is no difference between a long and a short rate as far as explanatory power is concerned. However, as far as postwar data, particularly for the United States, are concerned, we can be more definite, for studies of such data show that rates of return on close substitutes for money have played an important role in the function in recent years, although Hamburger (1966, 1977) has shown that the yield on corporate stock also affects the demand for money. Even so, when using a broad definition of money, Lee (1967) found the interest differential between time deposits and that on savings and loan association shares important and, in 1969, found that the yield on corporate equities supplemented rather than supplanted the influence of the rate of return on savings and loan association shares on the demand for narrow money. Goldfeld (1973) found the time deposit rate important when using a narrow definition of money, even when he also included a short-term market interest rate—that on 4- to 6-month commercial paper—in his equation. Cagan and Schwartz (1975), in comparing quarterly data for 1921–1931 and 1954–1971, found a rate of return on savings deposits (computed as an average of the rates of return offered on a variety of such assets) more important in the latter period.

These results are typical of the time series evidence reported by Feige and Pearce (1976) and confirm that generated by several studies of portfolio behavior, surveyed by Feige (1974), which show rates of return on money substitutes to exert a systematic influence on the demand for demand deposits and time deposits at commercial banks. The role of rates of return on money substitutes has not been so closely studied for other countries, but it is worth noting that the Bank of England (1970) found the rate of return on deposits with local authorities an important argument in the demand-for-money function for almost the same time period over which Laidler and Parkin (1970) obtained negative results with the treasury bill rate. Moreover, in his study of Norway, Teigen (1971) found the rate of return on savings deposits important, but that on government bonds unimportant.

The Role of Expected Inflation

The significance of the expected rate of inflation as a factor influencing the demand for money is well established. Although Cagan's (1956) study of European hyperinflations has recently been criticized by Jacobs (1975) for using statistical methods that exaggerated the closeness of the relationship between these variables, there is no reason to believe that Cagan's results are entirely a statistical artifact. Moreover, numerous other studies of rapid inflations, some using econometrics and some using less formal techniques, have all come to the conclusion that variations in the expected inflation rate systematically influence the demand for money. Studies have been made on the Confederacy (Lerner, 1956), a group of 16 Latin American countries (Vogel, 1974), Chile (Harburger, 1963, Deaver, 1970), Argentina (Diz, 1970), Brazil and South Korea (Campbell, 1970), Nationalist China (Hu, 1971), and the Weimar Republic (Frenkel, 1977), and Perlman (1970) has shown that cross-country variations in the proportion of a country's assets held in liquid form are related in a systematic fashion to cross-country variations in the expected inflation rate. Although early work on the United States by Friedman (1959) and Selden (1956) could not find any systematic influence of the rate of inflation on the demand for money, more recent studies by Shapiro (1973) and Goldfeld (1973) have found one in post-World War II data, regardless of whether the expected inflation rate is measured as a weighted average of past actual rates of inflation or, in the case of some of Goldfeld's work, generated from opinion survey data. Moreover, it is worth noting that Brown (1939), in his pioneering study of the demand for money in interwar Great Britain, found that variations in the inflation rate influenced the demand for idle balances, and that Melitz (1976), in a study of France, found the expected inflation rate a more important opportunity cost variable than any market interest rate.

Quite apart from all this, there is an overwhelming amount of indirect evidence on the issue. As we have seen, there can be no reasonable doubt that variations in rates of interest influence the demand for money, and in virtually every study carried out the rate of interest variable used has been the rate of return on a nominal asset. Economic theory suggests that such rates of return should vary systematically with the expected inflation rate, and a large body of empirical evidence, some of which is surveyed in Laidler and Parkin (1975), confirms that they in fact do. These two factors taken together thus imply the existence of an indirect, but nevertheless well determined, channel whereby variations in the expected inflation rate influence the demand for money. Because, for reasons not well understood, variations in nominal interest rates do not fully reflect variations in the expected inflation rate, this particular channel of causation still leaves room for the expected inflation rate to play a direct role in the demand-for-money function over and above that played by nominal interest rates as, for example, the results of Brown, Melitz, Shapiro, and Goldfeld show. All four found a role for the expected inflation rate in a function that also contains a nominal interest rate variable.

Finally, we note that Klein (1977) has investigated the possibility that *variations* in the inflation rate, by introducing extra uncertainty into the return to be had from holding money, hence lowering its "quality," may reduce the demand for money, or increase it. The rationale for the latter alternative, which Klein finds confirmed by the evidence, is that, when the quality of money is reduced by unpredictability as regards its future purchasing power, people choose to hold more of it in order to attain the desired level of services from their money holdings.†

The Influence of the Price Level

All the theories discussed in Chapters 4 and 5 involve the proposition that the demand for money balances measured in real terms is invariant with respect to the price level or, to put the same matter another way, that the demand for nominal balances is proportional to the price level. Many of the tests we have dealt with already in this chapter have taken this prediction for granted, and the demand-for-money functions fitted in the course of carrying them out have been cast in real terms. The original data on nominal wealth, income, and the money stock were divided through by the price level before being used for regression analysis. The reason for this is as follows. If the demand-for-money function under test is, say,

$$\frac{M_d}{P} = bX^{\beta_0}r^{\beta_1} \tag{7-8}$$

one of the pieces of information one requires from the regression is the value of the β's. If it is taken for granted that the demand for nominal balances is proportional to the price level, this function can be rewritten in nominal terms by multiplying both sides through by P; thus

$$M_d = bPX^{\beta_0}r^{\beta_1} \tag{7-9}$$

† For a discussion of theoretical statistical problems involved in distinguishing between the effects on the demand for money of the expected rate of inflation and its variability, see Eden (1976).

This is not the same function as

$$M_d = b(PX)^{\beta_0} r^{\beta_1} \tag{7-10}$$

which is what would be fitted if the data were left in nominal terms, for here β_0 would measure an average of the wealth, or income elasticity of demand for money and the price-level elasticity of the demand for money. The former can in principle, take any value, while in Equation (7-9) the latter is assumed to be equal to one.

If the price-level elasticity of the demand for money is equal to one, the estimate of the wealth or income elasticity of the demand for money coming from an expression like Equation (7-10) will be biased toward one.† In order to avoid such a bias, formulations like Equation (7-8) have generally been preferred for empirical work. This procedure is all right so long as one is convinced that the price-level elasticity of demand for money is indeed equal to one. If it is not, to divide an expression like

$$M_d = bP^{\beta_2} X^{\beta_0} r^{\beta_1} \qquad \beta_2 \neq 1 \tag{7-11}$$

through by P yields not Equation (7-8), but rather

$$\frac{M_d}{P} = bP^{(\beta_2 - 1)} X^{\beta_0} r^{\beta_1} \tag{7-12}$$

That is to say, if Equation (7-11) rather than Equation (7-9) is correct, the demand for real balances will also depend upon the level of

† To relate the nominal quantity of money demanded to some other variable valued at current prices can also produce a misleadingly close relationship between the variables. One tends to attribute to this other variable the effects of changes in the price level on the demand for nominal balances. This is a particularly important phenomenon at times of rapid inflation when most of the variation in the demand for nominal balances is due to changes in the price level, so that almost any variable one can name—provided its value also varies with the price level—appears to explain the demand for money. This factor probably accounts for the results reported by Allais (1966) for a demand-for-money equation using measured nominal income and omitting the rate of interest. They are markedly better for periods of hyperinflation than other times. It is difficult to assess the importance of the results of Allais, for he does not compare them to those obtained with other hypotheses. However, one should suspend judgment on this particular paper, since it represents a summary of a large amount of work available only in French. It may be that many of the comments one might offer are dealt with in these original papers.

prices, and the omission of this variable may show itself in instability and poorness of fit in any test that uses data measured in real terms. The fact that such instability has not appeared suggests strongly that the price-level elasticity of demand for money is indeed one, and that the price level does not influence the level of real-money holdings.

There is, however, more evidence than this available. Meltzer (1963) was not willing to take it for granted that the demand for nominal balances is proportional to the price level. He investigated this matter directly. First, he fitted functions (using wealth and income in different formulations) both to data cast in nominal terms and data cast in real terms. That is to say, he measured β_0 in the context both of an expression like Equation (7-8) and of an expression like Equation (7-10). His results show a distinct tendency for the estimate of β_0 to be closer to one in the latter case, as one would predict if the demand for nominal balances were proportional to the price level. Nor did Meltzer stop here; he went on to fit directly to the data a regression based on Equation (7-11), obtaining a direct estimate of β_2. The resulting estimate was, to all intents and purposes, equal to one.

In the course of studying postwar United States data, Goldfeld (1973) also directly investigated this matter. He included the price level in a demand-for-real-balances function and found that the elasticity of demand for real balances with respect to the price level was zero, thus confirming that the coefficient β_2 in Equation (7-11) indeed takes a value of unity. In their study of postwar British data, Laidler and Parkin (1970) followed essentially the same procedure as Meltzer and obtained similar results, while the Bank of England (1970) produced evidence suggesting that the demand for nominal balances varies in proportion to the price level but perhaps with a lagged response. In short, the direct evidence confirms what the indirect evidence suggests, namely, that economic theory is correct in asserting that the demand for money is a demand for real balances. The reader should note, however, that Jacobs (1974) has criticized, on econometric grounds, the work of Meltzer and Laidler and Parkin, so that there must remain some question about how strong the direct evidence is on this matter.

The Choice of a Scale Variable

We now come to the question of whether one should use income or some wealth variable in the demand-for-money function. The evidence here seems to be fairly strongly in favor of a wealth variable.

It was explained in the last chapter that two wealth concepts have been thought to be relevant to the demand for money. First, directly measured data on the value of assets in the United States economy have been aggregated to produce a series for nonhuman wealth owned in the economy. Second, permanent income, measured as an exponentially weighted average of current and past levels of net national product, has been employed as a proxy for a more inclusive concept which treats the present value of future labor income as part of the current stock of wealth. Either concept appears to be able to explain more of the variation in the demand for money than current income does. To deal with such an issue it is necessary to compare the performance of demand-for-money functions, identical except for the presence of wealth in one and income in the other, in the face of identical evidence and using identical statistical techniques. Such experiments have been carried out by Meltzer (1963), Brunner and Meltzer (1963), Laidler (1966a), and Chow (1966), using United States data.

Meltzer's basic technique was to perform regressions which contained both income and wealth variables, as well as regressions which contained each separately. He found, first, that wealth (nonhuman wealth in this case) provided a more stable demand-for-money function than income, and also that, if both variables were included in the function, wealth showed itself sufficiently closely related to the demand for money to leave nothing for income to explain. The latter variable turned out to be redundant in the presence of wealth. He also fitted one or two functions using permanent income and found that this variable too explained more than measured income did. These results appear to hold regardless of whether money is defined to include or exclude time deposits. Chow, for the period 1897–1959, fitted regressions using permanent income, measured income as alternatives, and found that, as far as the equilibrium demand for money was concerned, the former variable performed better.

Strong evidence that wealth or permanent income performs better than measured income as a scale variable in the United States demand-for-money function comes from Brunner and Meltzer's (1963) prediction tests mentioned earlier. They directly compared functions using income, nonhuman wealth, and permanent income and used both broad and narrow definitions of money. They found that, regardless of the definition of money used, functions using a wealth concept gave more accurate predictions of the velocity of circulation than those constrained by income. Just as important, they found that the superior predictive power of wealth was not just a matter of its having been particularly accurate over one short time span, but rather that it was consistently more accurate over the entire period from the beginning of this century.

Brunner and Meltzer's conclusion is strengthened by evidence produced by Laidler (1966a), using a rather different technique. Year-to-year changes in the data, rather than their annual levels were used in the tests, and nonhuman wealth was measured in a different indirect way. The change in the public's holding of wealth in any year must be equal to their saving. There is much evidence to suggest that consumption is a constant fraction of permanent income and, since saving is equal to income minus consumption, it should also be equal to measured income minus permanent income (a variable usually known as *transitory income*) plus a constant fraction (one minus the propensity to consume) of permanent income. Instead of a direct measure of a change in wealth then, two variables, transitory income and permanent income, were used in the regression and related to changes in money holding. The function fitted was a linear one, and the results achieved with it were compared with similar formulations of functions relating changes in the demand for money to changes in measured income and changes in permanent income.† A short rate of interest was included, and both broad and narrow definitions of money were employed. With either definition of money, wealth and expected income performed better than measured income, inasmuch as they produced functions that explained more of the variance in year-to-year changes in the demand for money.

Laidler (1971) also carried out tests on British data using measured- and permanent-income variables as alternatives and found that permanent income provided systematically better results, while Clark's (1973) work on Canada led to a similar conclusion. Diz's (1970) study

---

† One can put it symbolically thus. If

$$C = c Y^p$$
$$Y \equiv Y^p + Y^T$$

where Y^T is transitory income, then

$$S \equiv Y - C = Y^T + (1 - c) Y^p$$

(Note that since Y is national income, there is implicit here the assumption that the government debt is "inside" wealth.) Thus it was postulated that

$$\Delta M_d = b_0 Y^T + b_1 (1 - c) Y^p + b_2 \Delta r$$

This was the form the wealth function fitted. The time span of these tests was 1892–1960.

of Argentina generated evidence in favor of a permanent-income variable, though Deaver's (1970) work on Chile produced results that were indecisive in this respect.

The Scale Variable and Time Lags in the Function

All the above-cited evidence then, taken at face value, suggests that wealth rather than income belongs in the demand-for-money function, but there is one rather subtle point that needs looking at before we can come firmly to this conclusion.

The permanent-income series used in all the tests described here was generated by applying the error-learning hypothesis described in the previous chapter to data on measured income. Though the logarithm of permanent income measured in this way does not have quite the same value that would be obtained by taking a weighted average of past values of the logarithm of measured income—the former being the logarithm of a weighted average of incomes and the latter the weighted average of the logarithms of income—one would certainly be a good approximation of the other. Moreover, a priori there is no reason to prefer one way of generating a permanent-income series to another. Suppose we measure the logarithm of permanent income in the following way, with the roman (upright) Y standing for a logarithm [note: all variables standing for logarithms in Equations (7-13) through (7-24) are set in roman (upright) type]:

$$Y_t^p = \theta Y_t + (1 - \theta) Y_{t-1}^p \qquad (7\text{-}13)$$

Suppose also that we write the demand-for-money function in the following way, with M the log of real balances and R the log of the rate of interest:

$$M_t = \alpha + \beta_0 Y_t^p + \beta_1 R_t \qquad (7\text{-}14)$$

If we substitute Equation (7-13) into Equation (7-14), we will have

$$M_t = \alpha + \beta_0 \theta Y_t + \beta_0 (1 - \theta) Y_{t-1}^p + \beta_1 R_t \qquad (7\text{-}15)$$

An algebraic manipulation, known as the Koyck transformation after the econometrician who first applied it, enables us to eliminate the lagged permanent-income term in Equation (7-15) and to reduce it to a relationship between directly observable variables. Take Equation

(7-14), lag it one period, and multiply both sides of it by $(1-\theta)$ to obtain

$$(1-\theta)M_{t-1} = (1-\theta)\alpha + (1-\theta)\beta_0 Y^p_{t-1} + (1-\theta)\beta_1 R_{t-1} \qquad (7\text{-}16)$$

Subtract this expression from Equation (7-15). Evidently, the lagged permanent-income term disappears in this process, and the following expression is derived:

$$M_t = \theta\alpha + \beta_0 \theta Y_t + \beta_1 R_t - (1-\theta)\beta_1 R_{t-1} + (1-\theta)M_{t-1} \qquad (7\text{-}17)$$

Now consider an alternative formulation of the demand-for-money function. Let M^* be the log of the quantity of real balances people want to hold given the values of the variables that determine their demand for money, and let desired real balances be a log linear function of measured real income and the interest rate; thus

$$M^*_t = \alpha + \beta_0 Y_t + \beta_1 R_t \qquad (7\text{-}18)$$

However, suppose that, instead of cash balances adjusting instantaneously to their desired level when a variable on the right-hand side of the equation changes, the adjustment is slow and cash balances go only part of the way toward their newly desired values over a given time period. We can express this idea in the following equation:

$$M_t - M_{t-1} = \gamma(M^*_t - M_{t-1}) \qquad (7\text{-}19)$$

Substituting Equation (7-18) into Equation (7-19) enables us to write

$$M_t = \gamma\alpha + \beta_0\gamma Y_t + \beta_1\gamma R_t + (1-\gamma)M_{t-1} \qquad (7\text{-}20)$$

Before going any further, it is worth digressing briefly to point out that this analysis of an adjustment lag is not quite as straight-forward as it seems. It is plausible that a *single individual* might, because of the costs of rearranging his portfolio, adjust his money holdings slowly when their equilibrium value changes. However, when we come to the behavior of the *aggregate* demand for money in the *economy as a whole*, the following problem arises. If the quantity of *nominal* money is an exogenous variable, then the only way in which the quantity of *real* money can adjust slowly to equilibrium is by way of a slow adjustment of the general price level. We cannot explain slow adjustment in the aggregate demand for money in terms of the costs of adjusting portfolios faced by individuals. In short, if the nominal money supply is exogenous, we commit a fallacy of composition if we analyze the adjustment of the aggregate demand for real balances to equilibrium as if it were governed by the same forces that determine the adjustment of a single individual's money holdings to equilibrium. This point seems to have been made first by Walters (1965), but it has not been given the attention it deserves in subsequent work on the nature of the lags in the demand-for-money function. Only one published paper, by Artis & Lewis (1976), and one as yet unpublished paper, by Carr and Darby (mimeo, 1976), have attempted to pursue its implications. At present, we simply do not know whether this matter has important implications or not, and it is largely ignored in the rest of this chapter.

Whatever we may think about the significance of the matters just discussed, the important thing about the adjustment-lag hypothesis, for purposes of the present discussion, is that Equation (7-20), which we have derived from it, differs from Equation (7-17), yielded by the permanent-income hypothesis, only in the absence of a lagged interest rate variable. In the tests described above, the measured-income demand for money functions, which did not perform as well as those that used permanent income, contained no lagged value of the dependent variable. They were in fact special cases of Equation (7-20) with the parameter γ set equal to one. However, several workers, for example, Teigen (1964), de Leeuw (1965), and Bronfenbrenner and Mayer (1960) for the United States and Fisher (1968) for Great Britain included a lagged dependent variable in what they regarded as a measured-income formulation of the function and found it to play an important role. These results raise a serious problem. Could it be that the apparent superiority of permanent income in the demand-for-money function simply reflects the presence of adjustment lags in a function in which measured income is important? Though Equation (7-17) is not identical to Equation (7-20), it is sufficiently similar that, if one yields good results when applied to a particular body of data, so will the other, and it will be impossible to decide which is better without directly comparing the results they generated.

Feige (1967), following up the pioneering study of Chow (1966), set about resolving this problem in the following way. He reasoned that both expectation lags of the type postulated in Equation (7-13) and adjustment lags such as that described by Equation (7-19) can simultaneously be present in the demand-for-money function. Such a model can be written as follows:

$$M_t^* = \alpha + \beta_0 Y_t^p + \beta_1 R_t \qquad (7\text{-}21)$$

$$Y_t^p = \theta Y_t + (1 - \theta) Y_{t-1}^p \qquad (7\text{-}13)$$

$$M_t - M_{t-1} = \gamma(M_t^* - M_{t-1}) \qquad (7\text{-}19)$$

Appropriate substitutions and an application of the Koyck transformation enable us to derive the following expression from these equations:

$$M_t = \alpha\theta\gamma + \beta_0\theta\gamma Y_t + \beta_1\gamma R_t - \beta_1\gamma(1 - \theta)R_{t-1}$$
$$+ (2 - \gamma - \theta)M_{t-1} - (1 - \theta)(1 - \gamma)M_{t-2} \qquad (7\text{-}22)$$

A sophisticated statistical technique whose details need not concern us here enabled Feige to obtain estimates of the parameters of the basic model, α, β_0, β_1, γ, and θ. Using a narrow definition of money, and annual data for the United States for the period 1915–1963, he found that the parameter γ was just about equal to one, implying that no adjustment lag was present in the data but that the parameter λ took a value of about 0.4. The rather long expectation lag implicit in this estimate was completely consistent with the one generated by Friedman in his consumption function work and used in constructing the permanent-income series employed in earlier studies of the demand for money described above. In addition, Feige found that the permanent-income and interest elasticities of demand yielded by his study were completely consistent with those produced by earlier work. In short, his study provided striking confirmation of the superiority of permanent income over measured income as an argument in the demand-for-money function.

Feige's study is important not only because of the light it threw on the question of permanent income versus measured income as a scale variable in the demand-for-money function, but also because, in paying explicit attention to the modeling of time lags in the demand-for-money function, it opened up a whole new area of research in monetary economics. For example, Meyer and Neri (1975) recently developed Feige's analysis with a view to refining the notion of "expected income." We have seen that the error-learning hypothesis produces a series that is a geometrically weighted average of current and past income levels. Meyer and Neri argue, on the basis of statistical forecasting theory, that such a series is indeed a good representation of a "long-run normal" income level, and hence a good proxy variable for wealth. They also suggest that what we could call "short-term ex-pected" income should be distinguished from long-term normal or permanent income, that such a variable may be important in the demand-for-money function, and that it can be measured in the fol-lowing way. The value of permanent income at any moment is the value that people expect their actual income eventually to converge on, but there is no reason for them to expect that convergence to be immediate. If convergence is slow, short-term expected income will lie between current income and permanent income; the difference between expected income and current income will be a proportion of the difference between permanent income and current income. Thus, with the variables in logarithms, and Y^e as the log of short-term expected income we have

$$Y_t^e - Y_t = \delta(Y_t^p - Y_t) \tag{7-23}$$

so that

$$Y_t^e = \delta Y_t^p + (1 - \delta)Y_t \tag{7-24}$$

Meyer and Neri included expected income thus defined as a scale variable in the demand-for-money function fitted to annual United States data. A technique similar to that used by Feige enabled them to estimate the value of δ, along with the other parameters of the func-tion. Had the value of δ turned out to be one, this result would have implied that the expected-income variable is not operationally sig-nificant and that permanent income is the appropriate scale variable for the function; had it turned out to be equal to zero, the implication would have been that measured income is the appropriate scale vari-able. In fact, when a narrow definition of money was used, the value of δ turned out to be clearly between these extremes. Though it fell in the same range when a broad definition of money was used, it was in fact closer to one in this case. Thus, although Feige's work showed clearly that permanent income is a superior variable to measured income in the demand-for-money function, the work of Meyer and Neri shows that it is possible to do still better.

Feige's work found no room for an adjustment lag in the demand-for-money function, but he used annual data. His results imply that the demand for money adjusts virtually completely to interest rate variations within a year, but not to income variations, the slowness in response being attributed to the time it takes for income expectations to adapt to experience. Nevertheless, adjustment lags may play an important role in interpreting the behavior of money holdings averaged over shorter time periods. It is not surprising therefore that in the wake of Feige's work have come several studies dealing with essentially the same issues he raised but utilizing quarterly data and, in some cases (for example, Shapiro, 1973; Goldfeld, 1973), econometric techniques which permit somewhat more flexibility in dealing with lag patterns than is permitted by the particular formulations of the expectations and adjustment mechanisms used by Feige. The results of this work are encouragingly uniform. Shapiro and Goldfeld both found, for post-World War II United States data, that the demand for money is slower to respond to real income than to other variables. Laidler and Parkin (1970) applied Feige's techniques to quarterly British data for the years 1955–1967 and found evidence consistent with the presence of both expectation and adjustment lags in the demand-for-money function, the former probably being longer than the latter, though the difficulties they encountered in finding a role for the interest rate in the function (see p. 127) made their results on this issue difficult to interpret. [As the reader will see on inspecting Equation (7-22), to set the parameter β_1 equal to zero ensures that the parameters γ and θ enter completely symmetrically in Equation (7-22), making it impossible to distinguish between them.]

Earlier work on annual data (for example, Meltzer, 1963; Laidler, 1966a) provided no strong grounds for preferring permanent income to nonhuman wealth in the demand-for-money function, each variable performing about as well as the other, but Goldfeld's work on quarterly data casts more light on this choice. He showed that, once lagged responses to income are allowed for in the demand-for-money function, there is little in the way of explanatory power that nonhuman wealth can add, whether this power is assessed in terms of an equation's goodness of fit to a particular sample of data or in terms of its ability to forecast outside the sample period.

The results of all this work on the appropriate scale variable to include in the demand-for-money function are easily summarized. The evidence is overwhelming that current income is inadequate unless appropriate allowance is made for lags in the response of money holdings to variations in income. However, such a lagged response is plausibly interpreted as reflecting the adaptation of income expectations to experience, and hence points to the appropriateness of using some permanent- or expected-income variable in the function. Although much early work led to indecisive results concerning the choice between such a variable and nonhuman wealth, there is now evidence that nonhuman wealth has an inferior explanatory power.

The Role of the Wage Rate

As noted earlier in this chapter, only two studies have been carried out on the role of the wage rate, interpreted as a proxy variable for the brokerage fee of transactions and precautionary theories of the demand for money. The first of these studies, by Dutton and Gramm (1973), used United States annual data for the period 1919–1958 and also included an interest rate and nonhuman wealth in the function. A variety of alternative measures of wealth was employed, all of which differed from that employed by Meltzer in excluding government debt (see footnote on p. 105), and a variety of interest rate variables. The wage rate proved to have a systematic positive effect on the demand for money, regardless of precisely which other variables were included in the function. In Karni's (1974) study, data for a slightly longer time period (1919–1968) were used, and the model of the demand for money that underlay the empirical function was more closely related to an explicit inventory-theoretic approach to the demand for money. Here too, though, Karni found a wage variable (real hourly earnings) to have a systematic influence on the demand for money. Of course one would like to see the importance of the wage variable investigated across a far wider variety of specifications of the demand-for-money function than these before concluding definitely that the work of Dutton and Gramm and of Karni has unearthed another important factor influencing money holding, but the results they generated are nevertheless highly suggestive and open up an interesting line for future research.

Economies of Scale

Two issues remain to be dealt with—the existence of economies of scale in money holding and the most appropriate definition of money. The evidence on the first of these is somewhat mixed. If one looks at studies of long runs of United States annual data such as Friedman (1959), Laidler (1966b, 1971), and Meltzer (1963), or of long runs of British data such as Kavanagh and Walters (1966) and Laidler (1971), or of data for such countries as Chile (Hynes, 1967) and Argentina (Diz, 1970), one has the impression that economies of scale in money holding are nonexistent. Broader definitions of money on the whole produce higher estimates of the income or wealth elasticity of the demand for money than narrower ones, but it is a fair generalization to say that unity puts a lower bound upon the range of the estimates.

However, as already noted, several of these studies, and in particular some of those on the United States, also presented estimates of the demand-for-money function for subperiods, and these results seem to show that the elasticity in question has fallen over time. Thus Laidler's work (1971) using annual data for the United States suggests that the permanent-income elasticity of demand for money defined to include time deposits was 1.39 for the period 1900–1916, 1.28 for 1919–1940, and 0.65 for 1946–1965. For Great Britain, also using broad money, the relevant estimates were 1.24, 0.79, and 0.68 for the same time periods. These results are representative of a considerable body of evidence. Furthermore, studies using a narrow definition of money have found a more pronounced tendency for income or wealth elasticities of demand to lie below unity. In particular, the existence of economies of scale in the post-World War II demand-for-money function for both Great Britain and the United States is confirmed by several studies of quarterly data; see, for example, Shapiro (1973) and Goldfeld (1973) for the United States and Laidler and Parkin (1970) and the Bank of England (1970) for Great Britain. The results for 13 countries surveyed by Fase and Kure (1975) were all generated by postwar quarterly data and show a heavy preponderance of evidence that economies of scale exist. Such results arise no matter what definition of money is used and are not affected by the precise specification of the demand function fitted. Moreover, a less-than-unity income elasticity appears to characterize the demand-for-money functions of individual groups within the economy, for example, the household sector, as well as that of the economy as a whole. In short, though there is evidence enough that economies of scale in money holding are by no means universal, there can be little question that the demand-for-money functions of advanced economies, notably but by no means only those of Great Britain and the United States, have displayed such a property in the postwar period.

The Definition of Money

The evidence on the appropriate definition of money is somewhat mixed. There is no question that both broad and narrow definitions of money can be used successfully in studies of the demand for money, and as far as work dealing with long runs of annual time series data is concerned there seems to be little to choose between them. Thus, for example, Meltzer (1963), using nonhuman wealth and a long interest rate in the function, found a narrow definition of money to provide marginally more stable relationships, while Laidler (1966a, 1971), covering a very similar period but using permanent income and a short interest rate, found a broad definition to be slightly preferable. Meyer and Neri (1975) found their distinction between short-term expected and permanent income more important for narrowly than for broadly defined money. This evidence points toward a narrow definition of money as being more appropriate, because these results are consistent with the demand for demand deposits and time deposits arising from somewhat different motives.

Studies of portfolio behavior, pioneered by Christ (1963) and Feige (1964), many of which are surveyed by Feige (1974), have investigated this issue much more directly. Such work involves simultaneously fitting arrays of demand functions for a variety of assets and investigating the responsiveness of the demand for each asset to the rates of return on all other assets. If it really is the case that a broad definition of money is to be preferred to a narrow one, such studies should, in the context of the United States, reveal a degree of substitutability between demand deposits at commercial banks and time deposits (which are included in a broad definition of money but not in a narrow one) closer than that which exists between time deposits and such assets as mutual savings bank deposits and savings and loan association shares (which are usually excluded even from a broad money definition). As Feige's survey shows, the evidence of such studies is that there is a greater degree of substitutability between time deposits and these other assets than between demand deposits and time deposits, and hence points to a narrow definition of money as being more appropriate. One cannot accept these results as definitive, because most of them were generated by studies that treated variations in the ratio of service charges to the volume of demand deposits as a proxy for the own rate of return on demand deposits, and Klein's work on the competitive rate of return on money raises the suspicion that this proxy may not be an accurate one. How much difference the use of Klein's variable would make in the results in question cannot be settled a priori, and it would be interesting to have this matter investigated.

Goldfeld's work, already discussed in the context of the lag structure of the demand-for-money function, throws light on the question of the definition of money as well. Goldfeld notes that there are two ways of deriving an aggregate demand-for-broadly-defined-money function. First, one can fit such a function directly and, second, one can fit individual demand functions for the components of broad money and aggregate these functions. He then reasons that, if the first approach provides a better explanation of the behavior of broadly defined money, both in terms of within sample period fit and outside sample period forecasting ability, a broad definition of money is appropriate. His results show quite clearly that the behavior of the demand function for time deposits is sufficiently different from those for currency and demand deposits that it pays to fit separate functions to the components of broadly defined money in the exercise just described. Thus, his results, like those surveyed by Feige, point toward a narrow definition of money as being more appropriate, at least as far as United States data are concerned. For Great Britain, the issue has not been so carefully investigated, but it is interesting to note that, as Artis and Lewis (1976) show, it is much easier to find continuity in the structure of the demand function for narrowly defined money before and after the Competition and Credit Control changes in the monetary system of 1971 than in the structure of the demand for broadly defined money. However, for Canada, we have already noted that the existence of savings deposits on which checks can be drawn introduces an extra element into the question of how to define money, and at least one worker, Courchene (1976), drawing on part of his earlier work with Kelly (Courchene and Kelly, 1971), argues in favor of a broader definition of money for that economy. Similarly, for France, Melitz (1976) finds a broad definition more appropriate.

Goldfeld's study of the United States utilized quarterly data and paid particular attention to the lag structure of the function. One possible factor contributing to the lags in demand-for-money functions fitted to quarterly data may be the speed at which money holdings adjust to equilibrium, a factor not present in annual data if Feige's work is believed (but see pp. 143–144). These lags in turn are usually thought of as relating to the costs people face in changing their pattern of asset holding. If the costs of varying the volume of demand deposits differ from the costs of varying the volume of time deposits, one would expect the demand functions for these assets to differ for quarterly data, but to differ in a way that would not be apparent from the study of annual data in which such adjustment lags would be effectively averaged out. Therefore it may well be that there is no contradiction between the views that a narrow definition of money is to be preferred for quarterly data and that either a broad or a narrow definition is appropriate when annual data are analyzed.

This interpretation of the evidence points to another possibility. There is no reason to suppose that the costs of adjusting the pattern of asset holding are the same for all economic agents. Firms, for example, have easier access to capital markets than households, and hence find such adjustments cheaper to make. This suggests that, when dealing with quarterly data, it may be helpful to disaggregate over classes of agents as well as over assets. Price (1972) carried out such an exercise for British data on firm and household money holding and found that the two sectors behaved very differently, although he did have difficulty in finding a satisfactory model for the behavior of firms. Goldfeld (1973) tried a similar exercise for the United States but broke his data down into four sectors—household, business, financial, and state and local government. He obtained the same kind of results as Price but found the business and state and local government sectors difficult to model. Thus we have evidence that, when we deal with quarterly data, the very notion of a stable demand-for-money function for the economy as a whole is questionable. As one disaggregates over time, it becomes necessary to disaggregate over both assets and agents to obtain satisfactory results. This does *not* mean that the notion of a stable aggregate demand-for-money function is untenable, but it does suggest that it is more useful in interpreting movements of long-run averages of data than in dealing with detailed quarter-by-quarter, let alone month-by-month, variations.

Concluding Remark

We have now completed our survey of the evidence on the various questions concerning the demand-for-money function that we set out at the beginning of this chapter. It remains now to assess the significance of this evidence both for the theories of the demand for money discussed in Part II and for the macroeconomic framework described in Part I. These matters are the subject of the next, concluding, chapter of this book.

8

Some Tentative Conclusions

As we saw in the preceding chapter, by no means all the issues raised by various theories of the demand for money have been settled by the empirical work done to date, nor is it likely that all the relevant questions will ever be settled. To suggest that they will be would be to suggest that economists are likely to give up working on the theory of the demand for money, and this is hardly a likely eventuality. Nevertheless, as we have also seen, the evidence on certain questions appears to be strong enough for the answers to them to be regarded as fairly settled, so that it will now be helpful to discuss briefly the relevance of the empirical evidence considered in the last chapters both for the theories of the demand for money that underlie the tests that generated the evidence, and for the type of macroeconomic model described in Chapter 2, whose behavior depends so critically upon the nature of the demand-for-money function included in it. Let us first take up the questions relevant to theories of the demand for money.

Relevance of the Evidence for Theories of the Demand for Money

The basic question to be asked in this context is whether or not it pays to base a model of the demand for money on careful and explicit analysis of the motives that lead people to hold money. Let us consider the speculative motive first. This analysis does not seem to have produced anything in the way of predictions that are both unique to the approach in question and empirically important. This approach tells us that the rate of interest belongs in the demand-for-money function, but so does nearly every other piece of analysis we have considered, while its use of wealth as a scale variable for the demand-for-money function does not set it apart from simpler asset-demand approaches to the theory of the demand for money such as that of Friedman. As we have already seen, the very fact that there are certain assets whose capital value does not vary with the rate of interest but which pay a return to their holders at a rate higher than that borne by commercial bank liabilities—assets such as savings and loan association shares in the United States, building society deposits in Great Britain, or deposits with trust companies in Canada on which checks cannot be drawn, to give but three examples—suggests that speculative motives cannot dominate the demand for money. If they did, commercial bank liabilities, particularly demand deposits, would not be held in any large amount by the public when, from the point of view of satisfying this motive, apparently perfect substitutes exist that pay more interest.

Matters are different when it comes to theories of the transactions and precautionary demand for money. Several predictions specific to these approaches have been confirmed by at least some of the evidence discussed above. Though there have been only two studies of the matter—those of Dutton and Gramm and of Karni—it seems that wage levels, standing as a proxy for brokerage costs, play a role in the function; portfolio studies suggest that demand and time deposits at commercial banks are far from being perfect substitutes for one another, at least in the United States; and recent work, such as that of Goldfeld, finds that, when quarterly data are used, it pays to use separate equations to deal with the behavior of demand and time deposits, not to mention currency. This evidence all points to the conclusion that demand deposits are assets that yield to their holders services that are to a significant degree distinctive from those offered by other assets. It is tempting to conclude that their distinguishing characteristic is that they are a means of exchange and that transactions and precautionary motives therefore dominate the demand for money.

Not all the evidence points so obviously in this direction, however. Measured income, rather than permanent income or wealth, tends to be the scale variable associated with these approaches to the theory of the demand for money, and there can be little question that it is inferior to both of the alternatives. Also, the existence of economies of scale in the demand-for-money function, a key prediction of transactions and precautionary theories, appears to be a relatively recent phenomenon in the United States, being largely confined to the post-World War II period. If we are to conclude that explicit theorizing about transactions and precautionary motives for holding cash balances add to our understanding of the demand-for-money function, we must reconcile the predictions yielded by such theorizing with these awkward facts.

It is relatively easy to deal with the poor performance of measured income as a scale variable in the demand-for-money function, because there is a large arbitrary element in associating it with the transactions approach to money holding in the first place. At best, it is a proxy variable for the volume of transactions taking place over a particular time period, and there is no necessity that it be a better proxy than permanent income. Note in particular that theorizing about the precautionary demand for money stresses uncertainty about the timing of payments and receipts and focuses on the relationship between money holdings and the expected average value of transactions. We know from work on the consumption function that consumption plans relate to permanent rather than measured income. This fact certainly gives us grounds for interpreting permanent income as an appropriate scale variable to associate with the expected volume of expenditure, and hence with transactions and precautionary motives for holding money. Indeed, Feige (1967) interpreted it in just this way. The work of Meyer and Neri (1975) lends further weight to this line of reasoning, because they showed it to be fruitful to distinguish short-term income expectations from long-term ones and found the former to be particularly important as far as the demand for narrowly defined money is concerned. It is plausible that short-term expectations are more closely related to planned transactions than long-term expectations, and hence that the demand for assets that are a means of exchange is particularly closely related to them.

What of the frequent absence of economies of scale from the

demand-for-money function? There are two, complementary, ways in which such evidence can be reconciled with theorizing about transactions and precautionary motives. First, as Fried (1973) has argued, when an economy's income grows over time, two factors affecting the transactions and precautionary demand for money will vary. First, the planned volume of transactions will go up and, other things being equal, if money is held for transaction purposes, one would expect the ratio of money holdings to income to fall as a result of this. However, at the same time the level of wages will increase, and, as the opportunity cost of time thus rises, one would expect the volume of money holding associated with any planned volume of transactions to rise. These two forces will operate in opposite directions on the money/income ratio as an economy's income rises, and there is nothing to rule out the effect of rising wages, of an increasing brokerage fee, swamping the economies of scale associated with a growing transactions volume. The appropriate way to investigate this suggestion would be to include a wage rate variable as well as some other scale variable in the demand-for-money function in order to sort out their relative contributions to variations in money holding. We have seen that Dutton and Gramm did just this, and found that once a wage rate variable was included in the demand-for-money function the wealth elasticity of demand for money fell significantly below unity. Thus there is some empirical support for the foregoing line of reasoning.

Even so, the above argument does not account for the discrepancy between prewar and postwar results on the question of economies of scale, nor does it account for the steady downward drift over time of the permanent-income elasticity of demand for money that we noted in both British and United States demand functions. The most plausible explanation of these phenomena rests on the observation that, with the passage of time, the monetary systems of both countries have become more sophisticated. The recent growth of financial intermediaries whose liabilities may be regarded as close substitutes for money has often been noted, and we have seen that the rates of return on such assets have become more important as arguments in the demand-for-money function in postwar years. Cagan and Schwartz (1975), building upon a line of reasoning initially advanced by Marty (1961), have argued that one consequence of this growth of financial intermediaries has been a shift in emphasis within the pattern of motivation underlying money holding in the United States. When mutual savings banks, savings banks, and savings and loan associations were relatively unimportant, people held money not just for transactions and precautionary motives but also as a convenient way of storing wealth in a liquid form. Asset motives for holding money can just as easily be satisfied by holding the liabilities of financial intermediaries and, as these institutions have become important, there has been a transfer of funds to their liabilities, leaving money holding satisfying only transactions and precautionary motives. According to the above argument, it was only in the postwar period that money holding was mainly motivated by the transactions and precautionary considerations that lead to economies of scale in money holding.

A certain amount of other evidence tends to favor the foregoing analysis. Economies of scale began to appear in the British demand-for-money function during the interwar period, and the British financial system was more sophisticated than the United States one during that period, particularly as far as the development of nonbank financial intermediaries was concerned. Moreover, we have also seen that in certain countries where the financial structure is relatively less sophisticated, for example, Chile and Argentina, the income elasticity of demand for money is well above unity, suggesting that in these economies the motives underlying money holding encompass much more than transactions and precautionary considerations.

None of this evidence can be regarded as definitive, but it seems strong enough for us to argue that we should not allow the absence of economies of scale in money holding in earlier periods to persuade us to ignore the fact that theories based upon careful analysis of transactions and precautionary motives seem to yield important and unique insights into the behavior of the demand-for-money function, particularly for advanced economies in postwar years, and that such lines of theorizing are well worth further development.

Implications of the Evidence for Macroeconomics

If the conclusions one can draw about the theory of the demand for money are relatively tentative ones, it is possible to be a bit more definite about what we have learned about the macroeconomic model set out in Part I and its relevance to the actual economy. If it can for the moment be assumed that the other relationships in the economy are as they are there postulated—namely, that consumption depends upon the level of income and investment on the rate of interest, and that the money supply can be treated as exogenous—the findings about the relationship between the demand for money and the rate of interest set out above allow a major issue to be settled.

Neither of the extreme possibilities discussed in Chapter 2 turns out to have any empirical content. It is not true that the demand for money is unrelated to the rate of interest, nor does it seem to be the case that this function becomes perfectly elastic with respect to the rate of interest at any relevant level of the short rate. It follows from this that, in order to assess the effect that some given change in government expenditure, tax rates, or the money supply will have upon the economy, one must make use of a complete model of the economy and not concentrate solely on one sector of it.

However, the reader would be wrong to infer that the theories and evidence discussed in this book have led to no more than confirmation of the appropriateness of using an *IS-LM* model, with an upward sloping *LM* curve, for analyzing questions about the behavior of the aggregate economy. On the contrary, this work has played an important role in undermining the central position that such a model once held in macroeconomics. Perhaps the most obvious shortcoming of the *IS-LM* model when it is confronted with the evidence described in the last chapter is its comparative static nature. It deals with once-and-for-all changes in the equilibrium values of endogenous variables as they respond to changes in the values of exogenous variables. A key finding of virtually all the empirical work we have discussed is that, if we are to make sense of real-world data, we must allow for the fact that the demand for money responds with time lags to changes in the factors determining it. This result is particularly marked when we look at quarterly data, but the role that permanent- or expected-income variables play in studies of annual data implies that time lags are of basic importance there too. In this respect, empirical work on the demand for money echoes results generated by work on the consumption and investment functions.

The implications of all this evidence go far beyond the simple proposition that it "takes time" for the economy to move from one equilibrium to another. Indeed, such a proposition is potentially highly misleading. To see this, consider an (over)simplified model in which the demand for real balance depends only on real permanent income and in which the money supply is exogenous and the price level given. We can then write

$$\left(\frac{M_s}{P}\right)_t = \left(\frac{M_d}{P}\right)_t = m Y_t^p \qquad (8\text{-}1)$$

$$Y_t^p = bY_t + (1-b)\,Y_{t-1}^p \tag{8-2}$$

Substituting Equation (8-2) into Equation (8-1), applying the Koyck transformation, and rearranging gives

$$Y_t = \frac{1}{mb}\left(\frac{M_s}{P}\right)_t - \frac{1-b}{mb}\left(\frac{M_s}{P}\right)_{t-1} \tag{8-3}$$

Suppose that, in time t, the money supply is increased and thereafter held constant. The effect will be to increase Y_t by $1/mb$ times the change in M_s. But, because $M_{s_{t+1}} = M_{s_t}$, income in $t+1$ will be given by

$$Y_{t+1} = \frac{1}{mb}\left(\frac{M_s}{P}\right)_{t+1} - \frac{1-b}{mb}\left(\frac{M_s}{P}\right)_t = \frac{1}{m}\left(\frac{M_s}{P}\right)_t \tag{8-4}$$

and the change in income between $t-1$ and $t+1$ will be just $1/m$ times the change in the money supply. In short, when the money supply is changed in a model such as this, income initially changes by *more* than the ultimate amount. The effect of introducing a lag into the demand-for-money function is to speed up rather than slow down the economy's initial reaction to an exogenous change in the money supply, and for reasons that are obvious enough once we think about them. Equation (8-1) tells us that the level of permanent income must adjust to keep the supply and demand for money in equilibrium when the supply changes, but Equation (8-2) tells us that the only way in which, at time t, the level of permanent income can be changed is for current income to change by a greater amount. Thereafter, if there is no further change in the money supply, there can be no further change in permanent income, but Equation (8-4) implies that, for this to be the case, measured income must fall back to the new level of permanent income and remain there.

The foregoing analysis, based on the work of Walters (1965), was chosen for purely illustrative purposes; we have seen evidence enough that the rate of interest belongs in the demand-for-money function. If we take note of this factor, we have to look at the behavior of the rest of the economy to see how income will respond both in the short run and in the long run to a change in income, because in such a case the interest rate will also adjust to help keep the demand and supply of money in equilibrium. The extent to which the level of expenditure in the economy reacts to interest rate changes will in turn determine the manner in which the initial effects of a monetary change are spread between interest rate changes and output changes. If expenditure is relatively insensitive to interest rate changes and responds only slowly to them, most of the initial impact of a change in the quantity of money will be on the level of interest rates, with income changes coming only later. Moreover, in such a case the response of the economy to an exogenous shift in the money supply will be spread out over far more than the two periods of our simple example and may well involve a cycle in the time path of the endogenous variables rather than a smooth monotonic approach to equilibrium. It is not possible to develop these points further without explicit mathematical analysis, and the reader who is interested in following up this matter is referred to Appendix C.

Suffice it here to note that the analysis presented in Appendix C suggests that the characteristics of the time path the economy follows when moving between equilibria are of at least as much interest as the equilibria themselves, and that, if we wish to understand this time path, we must work in terms of a model of the economy as a whole rather than concentrating upon one segment of it or another.

Lagged responses to income changes are by no means the only dynamic characteristics of the demand-for-money function that our survey of the empirical evidence has brought to light. We have seen that economic theory predicts that the expected rate of inflation should influence the demand for money, and we have also seen that there is an overwhelming amount of empirical evidence that it in fact does so. The analysis of price-level behavior carried out in Chapter 2 totally ignored this factor. That analysis predicted, given that output is fixed at an exogenous full-employment level, that the price level would move in proportion to the quantity of money. It would be a short step from this result to the conclusion that the inflation rate—the percentage rate of change of the price level—always equals the percentage rate of growth of the money supply but, in light of the evidence we have just cited, such a conclusion would be a misleading oversimplification.

It is certainly true that, if real balances are to remain constant while the nominal quantity of money grows, the price level must rise at the same rate as the quantity of money. Thus, holding real balances constant, an increase in the rate of monetary expansion will lead to an equal increase in the inflation rate. However, if the demand for real balances is inversely related to the expected rate of inflation, and if the expected rate of inflation varies with the current rate, it is not valid to assume that real balances remain constant when the rate of monetary expansion, and hence the inflation rate, increases. They will fall, so that, for a while after the increase in the rate of monetary expansion, prices will rise more rapidly than nominal balances. It is only when real balances have fallen to a level compatible with an inflation rate equal to the new rate of monetary expansion that such an equilibrium inflation rate can in fact be generated. There is no a priori reason to suppose that the time that must elapse for such a state of affairs to be reached will be short, or that the path by which the inflation rate approaches its long-run equilibrium value after initially overshooting it will be smooth and monotonic. It could well be cyclical. To generate the foregoing results more formally again requires explicit mathematical analysis, and such an analysis is presented in Appendix C. The basic implication of the analysis once again is that the time path the economy describes in approaching a new equilibrium is at least as interesting as the equilibrium itself.

The work on the demand-for-money function we described in the last chapter is only one of several factors that have forced economists to reassess the central role accorded the comparative static IS-LM model in macroeconomics. As noted, empirical work on consumption and investment behavior has also pointed to the importance of dynamic factors, as has work designed to investigate the way in which real output and employment on the one hand, and price and money wage levels on the other, interact over time. Such interaction, though a salient feature of any actual economy, is absent from the IS-LM framework as usually presented. But it has not just been empirical work that has undermined this once dominant orthodoxy. The actions of firms and households, when they are forced to take, at a particular moment, decisions that will commit them to a certain line of behavior in an uncertain future, have come in for much theoretical investigation in recent years, at both the micro and macro levels. The role of expectations in decision making is of central importance to such analysis, both from the point of view of how expectations influence behavior and of how expectations change in response to experience, but the role of expectations is ignored in the IS-LM model presented in Part I.

We came across bits and pieces of this theoretical work on expectations in Part II. The introduction of expected income and the expected inflation rate as arguments of the demand-for-money function are examples of this but, more fundamentally, it should be noted that the precautionary and speculative motives for money holding cannot be conceived of in the absence of uncertainty about the future. The speculative motive does not seem to tell us much about the demand for money, but this does not mean that it is not highly relevant to an understanding of the demand for other assets. However, in the context of the demand for money, the precautionary motive seems to have some empirical content. This is perhaps just as well, since the theoretical work to which we refer here suggests that, in the absence of uncertainty about the future, there cannot exist a demand for money in any economy.

Even so, the bulk of the theoretical work to which we are referring here has been concerned with the interaction of inflation and unemployment rather than the demand for money. It is now in the process of developing a much more subtle analysis of the processes whereby expectations are formed than the mechanical error-learning hypothesis underlying so much of the work surveyed in this book. Thus, the work of Brock (1972), Lucas (1972), and Sargent and Wallace (1975) rests on the *rational expectations hypothesis*, which states that maximizing agents will form their expectations by using "relevant" economic theory, rather than rules of thumb. It has developed a much more subtle analysis—whose technical difficulty puts it far beyond the scope of this book—of the way in which monetary factors impinge upon behavior than anything we have dealt with here. Such theoretical investigations have hardly yet borne fruit as far as increasing the sophistication and range of empirically testable hypotheses about the demand for money, though Frenkel (1977) represents a pioneering application of these ideas to the area; but it is hard to believe that they will not eventually produce many studies such as this. Thus the theories and empirical results surveyed in this book are inevitably interim in nature. They form part of a wider body of work which has led to the undermining of the very analytic framework in terms of which the work that produced them was initially cast, but an alternative framework has not yet been developed. Until it is, any firm assessment of the significance of recent theoretical and empirical work on the demand for money for macroeconomics is impossible, for the simple reason that we cannot be sure what shape the macroeconomic theory of the near future will take.

C

Two Dynamic Macromodels

An IS-LM Model with Expectation and Adjustment Lags

There is a substantial literature on the role of expectation and adjustment lags in a dynamic *IS-LM* framework. Relevant articles include Tucker (1966), Laidler (1968), Grossman and Dolde (1969), and Tanner (1969). The following model is the most general of those available and was first presented in Laidler (1973), where it is analyzed in much more detail than we have space for here.

The underlying framework of this model is the same as that presented in Appendix A. However, consumption and investment are aggregated into a single expenditure variable E, taxes are assumed equal to zero for the sake of simplicity, and the price level is set and held equal to unity so that M refers to real balances. In addition, Y is real income, Y^p is permanent income, G is government expenditure, r is the rate of interest, and a superscript asterisk denotes the planned value of a variable. In this model planned expenditure depends upon

163

permanent income and the rate of interest, but its achievement is subject to an adjustment lag; planned money holdings depend on the same variables, but once more are subject to an adjustment lag; the usual equilibrium conditions are imposed on the real-goods and money markets; and permanent income is generated by an error-learning mechanism. Thus, we can write

$$E_t^* = A + cY_t^p - ir_t \tag{C-1}$$

$$E_t = gE_t^* + (1-g)E_{t-1} \tag{C-2}$$

$$Y_t = E_t + G_t \tag{C-3}$$

$$M_t^* = mY_t^p - Ir_t \tag{C-4}$$

$$M_s = M_t = dM^* + (1-d)M_{t-1} \tag{C-5}$$

$$Y_t = bY_t + (1-b)Y_{t-1}^p \tag{C-6}$$

Substituting Equation (C-6) into Equations (C-1) and (C-4), eliminating the lagged expected-income variable by appropriate use of the Koyck transformation, substituting the resulting expressions into Equations (C-2), (C-3), and (C-5), and solving for Y_t yields

$$Y_t = \frac{1}{1-bgz}G_t - \frac{2-b-g}{1-bgz}G_{t-1} + \frac{(1-b)(1-g)}{1-bgz}G_{t-2} + \frac{g}{1-bgz}A_t$$

$$- \frac{(1-b)g}{1-bgz}A_{t-1} + \frac{1}{\frac{I}{i}\frac{d}{g}(1-bgz)}M_t - \frac{2-b-d}{\frac{I}{i}\frac{d}{g}(1-bgz)}M_{t-1}$$

$$+ \frac{(1-b)(1-g)}{\frac{I}{i}\frac{d}{g}(1-bgz)}M_{t-2} + \frac{2-b-g}{1-bgz}Y_{t-1} - \frac{(1-b)(1-g)}{1-bgz}Y_{t-2} \tag{C-7}$$

where

$$Z \equiv c - \frac{i}{I}m \tag{C-8}$$

The long-run equilibrium value of income $\bar{Y}$, which is reached when actual and permanent income are equal to each other and planned expenditure and planned money holdings are actually realized, is given by

$$\bar{Y} = \frac{1}{1-z}(G_t + A_t) + \frac{1}{\frac{I}{i}(1-z)}M_t \tag{C-9}$$

which the reader will recognize as the solution for income of the static *IS-LM* framework.

The behavior of the deviation of income from its long-run equilibrium value is given by the difference equation

$$(Y_t - \overline{Y}) - \alpha_1 (Y_{t-1} - \overline{Y}) + \alpha_2 (Y_{t-2} - \overline{Y}) = 0 \qquad \text{(C-10)}$$

where

$$\alpha_1 = \frac{2 - b - g}{1 - bgz} \qquad \alpha_2 = \frac{(1 - b)(1 - g)}{1 - bgz}$$

This deviation will converge on zero, that is to say, income will eventually reach its long-run equilibrium value if

$$\alpha_1 - \alpha_2 - 1 < 0$$

$$-\alpha_1 - \alpha_2 - 1 - < 0$$

and

$$\alpha_2 < 1$$

The last two of these inequalities are obviously satisfied for the model under analysis, because b, c, d, and g are fractions, and because z is less than unity. The first can be written as

$$\frac{2 - b - g}{1 - bgz} - \frac{(1 - b)(1 - g)}{1 - bgz} - 1 = \frac{bgz - bg}{1 - bgz} < 0 \qquad \text{(C-11)}$$

and this too is always satisfied, so that income always converges on its equilibrium value eventually.

Whether or not an equation of the form of Equation (C-10) converges upon zero monotonically or cyclically depends upon the properties of its roots, call them $x_1 x_2$. These are given by

$$x_1 x_2 = \frac{1}{2} \left[\frac{2 - b - g}{1 - bgz} \pm \sqrt{ \left(\frac{2 - b - g}{1 - bgz} \right)^2 - \frac{4(1 - b)(1 - g)}{1 - bgz} } \right] \qquad \text{(C-12)}$$

If the expression under the square-root sign is negative, this implies that the model displays cyclical behavior.

Now,

$$\left(\frac{2-b-g}{1-bgz}\right)^2 - \frac{4(1-b)(1-b)(1-g)}{1-bgz} = \frac{(b-g)^2+4(1-b)(1-g)bgz}{(1-bgz)^2}$$

(C-13)

and all terms but the last term in the numerator of this expression, as well as its denominator, are necessarily positive. The last term in the numerator, however, can be negative, because z can be negative, and it can be sufficiently large in absolute value to make the whole expression negative. Thus a cyclical disequilibrium time path from income is a possibility inherent in this model.

In Walter's very simple model, dealt with in the text, income overshoots its ultimate value in its initial response to a change in the money supply. We can investigate the existence of such overshoot effects in response to both money supply and government expenditure changes in this more complex model by comparing the sizes of the impact multipliers of these variables—the coefficients of M_t and G_t in Equation (C-7)—with those of the same variables in Equation (C-9). Let us compare the impact on the steady-state multipliers by computing the ratio of the latter to the former. Denoting these ratios by L_M for money and L_G for government expenditure, we have

$$L_M = \frac{d}{g}\frac{(1-bgz)}{1-z}$$

(C-14)

$$L_G = \frac{1-bgz}{1-z}$$

(C-15)

The second of these will be less than one, implying an overshoot effect in the economy's response to a change in government expenditure, if z is negative. The former will tend to be a fraction if z is negative, but the ratio d/g also enters into account here. A sufficiently small value of g relative to d will cancel out the effects of a negative value of z, implying that a long lag in the reaction of expenditure to interest rates works against overshooting as a characteristic of the economy's response to money supply changes.

The reader should note that many of the model's dynamic characteristics depend upon the conglomerate parameter z and should recall that

$$z \equiv c - \frac{i}{l}m$$

(C-8)

The sign of z is critically dependent upon the value of the ratio i/l, and this is of course the ratio of the slopes of the expenditure and demand-for-money functions with respect to the interest rate, the same ratio that, in the static *IS-LM* model, determines the relative importance of monetary and fiscal policy. Thus the foregoing analysis tells us that an economy in which money is relatively powerful is also prone to overshoots and cyclical behavior, while one in which fiscal policy is relatively powerful is characterized by less complicated dynamic behavior.

A Dynamic Model of Inflation

The following model derives from the work of Cagan (1956), but the discrete-time formulation used here follows Dutton (1971). Consider an economy in which the demand for real-money balances depends on the level of real income (or permanent income) and the expected rate of inflation, the latter being given by an error-learning process. Fix the level of real income at an exogenously given full-employment level and specify the demand-for-money function so that the log of real-money balances at time t, $M_t - P_t$, depends upon the log of (constant) real income Y and the level of the expected rate of inflation that ruled at the end of period $t-1$, ΔP^e_{t-1} Thus

$$M_t - P_t = w + kY - a\Delta P^e_{t-1} \qquad \text{(C-16)}$$

Note that the first difference in the log of the price level, ΔP_t, is equal to the proportional change in the price level that takes place between period $t-1$ and period t and defines the expected rate of inflation as

$$\Delta P^e_t = h\Delta P_t + (1-h)\Delta P^e_{t-1} \qquad \text{(C-17)}$$

Substituting Equation (C-17) into Equation (C-16), performing the Koyck transformation, and rearranging the result yields

$$P_t = hw + hkY + M_t - (1-h)M_{t-1} + (1-h+ah)P_{t-1} - ahP_{t-2} \qquad \text{(C-18)}$$

and, because the rate of change of real income is assumed equal to zero, the first difference of Equation (C-18) gives

$$\Delta P_t = \Delta M_t - (1-h)\Delta M_{t-1} + (1-h+ah)\Delta P_{t-1} - ah\Delta P_{t-2} \qquad \text{(C-19)}$$

For a constant rate of change in the nominal money supply, the rate of inflation in long-run equilibrium, when ΔP_t equals ΔP_{t-1} and ΔP_{t-2}, reduces to

$$\Delta P = \Delta M \qquad \text{(C-20)}$$

In long-run equilibrium the rate of inflation is equal to the rate of monetary expansion.

Applying the same rules concerning the stability of difference equations that we utilized in dealing with the previous model, we see that an economy such as we are considering will converge on this inflation rate if

$$(1 - h + ah) - ah - 1 < 0$$

$$-(1 - h + ah) - ah - 1 < 0$$

and

$$ah < 1$$

Clearly, the first two conditions will always be satisfied, the second because h is less than unity. h being a fraction will also help the third condition to be satisfied, but the sensitivity of the demand for money to the expected inflation rate, captured in the parameter a, could be large enough to cause the inflationary process to be self-generating and explosive. The empirical evidence we have on this issue, however, is consistent with the inflationary process being stable. The roots of the equation $x_1 x_2$ are given by

$$x_1 x_2 = \frac{1}{2} [1 - h + ah \pm \sqrt{(1 - h + ah)^2 - 4ah} \qquad \text{(C-21)}$$

Since

$$(1 - h + ah)^2 - 4ah = 1 + ah \left[\frac{h}{a} + ah - 2 \left(1 + h + \frac{1}{a} \right) \right] \qquad \text{(C-22)}$$

a cyclical time path for the inflation rate is a possibility.

Note that Equation (C-19) tells us that the impact effect in period t of an increase in the rate of monetary expansion is to increase the inflation rate by the same amount. In the next period, however, the coefficients of ΔM_{t-1} and ΔP_{t-1} become relevant. They push in opposite directions but, because the latter is larger in absolute value, the inflation rate continues to rise in the next period, thus overshooting its long-run equilibrium value.

Perhaps the most important implication of this model is that it shows the inflation rate to be equal to the rate of monetary expansion only in long-run equilibrium. Thus failure to observe equality between the inflation rate and the monetary expansion rate in the real world in no sense negates a monetary explanation of inflation.

References

Adekunle, J. O. 1968. "The Demand for Money: Evidence from Developed and Less Developed Economies," *I.M.F. Staff Papers*, 15 (July), 220–266.

Allais, M. 1966. "A Restatement of the Quantity Theory of Money," *American Economic Review*, 56 (December), 1123–1157.

Artis, M. J. and Lewis, M. K. 1976. "The Demand for Money in the United Kingdom, 1963–1973," *Manchester School*, 44 (June), 147–181.

Bank of England. 1970. "The Importance of Money," *Bank of England Quarterly Bulletin*, 10 (June), 159–198.

Barro, R. J. and Santomero, A. J. 1972. "Household Money Holdings and the Demand Deposit Rate," *Journal of Money, Credit and Banking*, 4 (May), 397–413.

Baumol, W. J. 1952. "The Transactions Demand for Cash: An Inventory Theoretic Approach," *Quarterly Journal of Economics*, 66 (November), 545–556.

Brock, W. 1972. "On Models of Expectations that Arise from Maximizing Behavior of Individuals over Time," *Journal of Economic Theory*, (December), 348–376.

Bronfenbrenner, M. and Mayer, T. 1960. "Liquidity Functions in the American Economy," *Econometrica*, 28 (October), 810–834.

Brown, A. J. 1939. "Interest, Prices and the Demand for Idle Money," *Oxford Economic Papers*, 2 (May), 46–69.

Brunner, K. and Meltzer, A. H. 1963. "Predicting Velocity: Implications for Theory and Policy," *Journal of Finance*, 18 (May), 319–354.

——. 1964. "Some Further Evidence on Supply and Demand Functions for Money," *Journal of Finance*, 19 (May), 240–283.

——. 1967. "Economies of Scale in Cash Balances Reconsidered," *Quarterly Journal of Economics*, 81 (August), 422–436.

Cagan, P. 1956. "The Monetary Dynamics of Hyperinflation," in M. Friedman (ed.), *Studies in the Quantity Theory of Money* (Chicago: University of Chicago Press).

Cagan, P. and Schwartz, A. J. 1975. "Has the Growth of Money Substitutes Hindered Monetary Policy," *Journal of Money, Credit and Banking*, 7 (May), 137–160.

Campbell, C. D. 1970. "The Velocity of Money and the Rate of Inflation: Recent Experience in South Korea and Brazil," in D. Meiselman (ed.), *Varieties of Monetary Experience* (Chicago: University of Chicago Press).

Carr, J. and Darby, M. R. 1976. "The Role of Money Supply Shocks in the Short-Run Demand for Money," University of California at Los Angeles (mimeo).

Chow, Gregory. 1966. "On the Long-Run and Short-Run Demand for Money," *Journal of Political Economy*, 74 (April), 111–131.

Christ, C. F. 1963. "Interest Rates and Portfolio Selection among Liquid Assets in the U.S.," in C. F. Christ et al., *Measurement in Economics: Essays in Mathematical Economics and Econometrics in Memory of Yehuda Grunfeld* (Stanford, Calif.: Stanford University Press).

Clark, C. 1973. "The Demand for Money and the Choice of a Permanent Income Estimate: Some Canadian Evidence 1926–1965," *Journal of Money, Credit and Banking*, 5 (August), 773–793.

Clinton, K. 1973. "The Demand for Money in Canada 1955–1970: Some Single-Equation Estimates and Stability Tests," *Canadian Journal of Economics*, 6 (February), 53–61.

Courchene, T. J. 1976. *Money and Inflation: An Evaluation of Recent Canadian Monetary Policy* (Montreal: C. D. Howe Research Institute).

Courchene, T. J. and Kelly, A. K. 1971. "Money Supply and Money Demand: An Econometric Analysis for Canada," *Journal of Money, Credit and Banking*, 3 (May), 219–243.

Crouch, R. L. 1971. "Tobin vs. Keynes on Liquidity Preference," *The Review of Economics and Statistics*, 53 (November), 368–371.

Deaver, J. V. 1970. "The Chilean Inflation and the Demand for Money," in D. Meiselman (ed.), *Varieties of Monetary Experience* (Chicago: University of Chicago Press).

DeLeeuw, F. 1965. *The Demand for Money, Speed of Adjustment, Interest Rates and Wealth*, Staff Economic Studies, Board of Governors of the Federal Reserve System, Washington, D.C.

Diz, A. C. 1970. "Money and Prices in Argentina 1935–62," in D. Meiselman (ed.), *Varieties of Monetary Experience* (Chicago: University of Chicago Press).

Dutton, D. S. 1971. "The Demand for Money and the Price Level," *Journal of Political Economy*, 79 (September-October), 1161–1170.

Dutton, D. S. and Gramm, W. P. 1973. "Transactions Costs, the Wage Rate, and the Demand for Money," *American Economic Review,* 63 (September), 652–665.

Eden, B. 1976. "On the Specification of the Demand for Money: The Real Rate of Return versus the Rate of Inflation," *Journal of Political Economy,* 84 (December), 1353–1360.

Edgeworth, F. Y. 1888. "The Mathematical Theory of Banking," *Journal of the Royal Statistical Society,* 51, 113–127.

Eisner, R. 1971. "Non-linear Estimates of the Liquidity Trap," *Econometrica,* 39 (September), 861–864.

Fase, M. M. G. and Kure, J. B. 1975. "The Demand for Money in Thirteen European and Non-European Countries: A Tabular Survey," *Kredit und Kapital,* 3, 410–419.

Feige, E. 1964. *The Demand for Liquid Assets: A Temporal Cross Section Analysis* (Englewood Cliffs, N.J.: Prentice-Hall).

——. 1967. "Expectations and Adjustments in the Monetary Sector," *American Economic Review,* 57 (May), 462–473.

——. 1974. "Alternative Temporal Cross-Section Specifications of the Demand for Demand Deposits," in H. G. Johnson and A. R. Nobay (eds.), *Issues in Monetary Economics* (London: Oxford University Press).

Feige, E. L. and Pearce, D. K. 1976. "Substitutability between Money and Near Monies: A Survey of the Time Series Evidence," SSRI Workshop Series 7617, University of Wisconsin, Madison, Wisc. (mimeo).

Fisher, D. 1968. "The Demand for Money in Britain: Quarterly Results 1951 to 1967," *Manchester School,* 36 (December), 329–344.

Fisher, I. 1911. *The Purchasing Power of Money* (New York: Macmillan).

Frenkel, J. 1977. "The Forward Exchange Rate, Expectations and the Demand for Money: The German Hyperinflation," *American Economic Review* (forthcoming).

Fried, J. 1973. "Money, Exchange and Growth," *Western Economic Journal,* 11 (September), 285–301.

Friedman, M. 1956. "The Quantity Theory of Money, A Restatement," in M. Friedman (ed.), *Studies in the Quantity Theory of Money* (Chicago: University of Chicago Press).

——. 1957. *A Theory of the Consumption Function* (Princeton, N.J.: Princeton University Press for the NBER).

——. 1959. "The Demand for Money—Some Theoretical and Empirical Results," *Journal of Political Economy,* 67 (June), 327–351.

——. 1966. "Interest Rates and the Demand for Money," *Journal of Law and Economics,* 9 (October).

Frowen, S. F. and Arestis, P. 1976. "Some Investigations of Demand and Supply Functions for Money in the Federal Republic of Germany 1965–74," *Weltwirtschaftliches Archiv,* 112, 136–164.

Gray, M. R. and Parkin, J. M. 1973. "Portfolio Diversification as Optimal Precautionary Behaviour," in M. Morishima, et al., *Theories of Demand, Real and Monetary* (London: Oxford University Press).

Gray, M. R., Ward, R. J., and Zis, G. 1976. "World Demand for Money," in J. M. Parkin and G. Zis (eds.), *Inflation in the World Economy* (Manchester: University of Manchester Press).

Goldfeld, S. M. 1973. "The Demand for Money Revisited," *Brookings Papers on Economic Activity,* 3, 577–638.

Goldman, S. M. 1974. "Flexibility and the Demand for Money," *Journal of Economic Theory*, 9 (October), 203–222.

Grossman, H. I. and Dolde, W. C. 1969. "The Appropriate Timing of Monetary Policy," Brown University, Providence, R.I. (mimeo).

Hamburger, M. J. 1966. "The Demand for Money by Households, Money Substitutes and Monetary Policy," *Journal of Political Economy*, 74 (December), 600–623.

———. 1977. "The Behavior of the Money Stock—Is There a Puzzle?" *Journal of Monetary Economics* (forthcoming).

Harburger, A. C. 1963. "The Dynamics of Inflation in Chile," in C. F. Christ et al., *Measurement in Economics: Essays in Mathematical Economics and Econometrics in Memory of Yehuda Grunfeld* (Stanford, Calif.: Stanford University Press).

Hicks, J. R. 1935. "A Suggestion for Simplifying the Theory of Money," *Economica*, 2 (February), 1–19.

Hu, T. W. 1971. "Hyperinflation and the Dynamics of the Demand for Money in China 1945–1949," *Journal of Political Economy*, 79 (January-February), 186–195.

Hynes, A. 1967. "The Demand for Money and Monetary Adjustments in Chile," *Review of Economic Studies*, 34 (July), 285–294.

Jacobs, R. L. 1974. "Estimating the Long-Run Demand for Money from Time Series Data," *Journal of Political Economy*, 82 (November-December), 1221–1238.

———. 1975. "A Difficulty with Monetarist Models of Hyper-inflation," *Economic Inquiry*, 13 (September), 332–360.

Johnson, H. G. 1963. "Notes on the Theory of Transactions Demand for Cash," *Indian Journal of Economics*, 44, part 1, no. 172 (July), 1–11.

———. 1969. "Inside Money, Outside Money, Income Wealth and Welfare in Monetary Theory," *Journal of Money, Credit and Banking*, 1 (February), 30–45.

Karni, E. 1974. "The Value of Time and the Demand for Money," *Journal of Money, Credit and Banking*, 6 (February), 45–64.

Kavanagh, N. J. and Walters, A. A. 1966. "The Demand for Money in the United Kingdom 1877–1961: Preliminary Findings," *Bulletin of the Oxford University Institute of Economics and Statistics*, 28 (May), 93–116.

Keynes, J. M. 1923. *A Tract on Monetary Reform* (London: Macmillan).

———. 1930. *A Treatise on Money* (London and New York: Macmillan, 1930).

———. 1936. *The General Theory of Employment, Interest, and Money* (London and New York: Macmillan).

Khan, M. 1974. "The Stability of the Demand for Money Function in the U.S. 1901–1965," *Journal of Political Economy*, 82 (November-December), 1205–1220.

Khusro, A. M. 1952. "An Investigation of Liquidity Preference," *Yorkshire Bulletin of Economic and Social Research*, 4 (January), 1–20.

Klein, B. 1974a. "The Competitive Supply of Money," *Journal of Money, Credit and Banking*, 6 (November), 423–454.

———. 1974b. "Competitive Interest Payments on Bank Deposits and the Long-Run Demand for Money," *American Economic Review*, 64 (December), 931–949.

——. 1975. "Our New Monetary Standard: The Measurement and Effects of Price Uncertainty 1880–1973," *Economic Inquiry*, 13 (December), 461–484.

——. 1977. "The Demand for Quality Adjusted Cash Balances: Price Uncertainty in the U.S. Demand for Money Function," *Journal of Political Economy* (forthcoming).

Kliman, M. L. and Oksanen, E. H. 1973. "The Keynesian Demand for Money Function: A Comment," *Journal of Money, Credit and Banking*, 5 (February), 215–220.

Kostas, P. and Khouja, M. W. 1969. "The Keynesian Demand for Money Function: Another Look and Some Additional Evidence," *Journal of Money, Credit and Banking*, 1 (November), 765–777.

Laidler, D. 1966a. "Some Evidence on the Demand for Money," *Journal of Political Economy*, 74 (February), 55–68.

——. 1966b. "The Rate of Interest and the Demand for Money—Some Empirical Evidence," *Journal of Political Economy*, 74 (December), 545–555.

——. 1968. "The Permanent Income Concept in a Macroeconomic Model," *Oxford Economic Papers*, 20 (March), 11–23.

——. 1969. "The Definition of Money: Theoretical and Empirical Problems," *Journal of Money, Credit and Banking*, 1 (August), 508–525.

——. 1971. "The Influence of Money on Economic Activity: A Survey of Some Current Problems," in G. Clayton, J. C. Gilbert, and R. Sedgwick (eds.), *Monetary Theory and Policy in the 1970s* (London: Oxford University Press).

——. 1973. "Expectations, Adjustment and the Dynamic Response of Income to Policy Changes," *Journal of Money, Credit and Banking*, 4 (February), 157–172.

Laidler, D. and Parkin, J. M. 1970. "The Demand for Money in the United Kingdom 1956–1967: Preliminary Estimates," *Manchester School*, 38 (September), 187–208.

Laidler, D. and Parkin, J. M. 1975. "Inflation—A Survey," *Economic Journal*, 85 (December), 741–809.

Latané, H. A., "Cash Balances and the Interest Rate—A Pragmatic Approach," *Review of Economics and Statistics*, 36 (November), 456–460.

Lee, T. H. 1967. "Alternative Interest Rates and the Demand for Money: The Empirical Evidence," *American Economic Review*, 57 (December), 1168–1181.

——. 1969. "Alternative Interest Rates and the Demand for Money—Reply," *American Economic Review*, 59 (June), 412–417.

Leponiemi, A. 1966. *On the Demand and Supply of Money: The Evidence from the Quarterly Time Series in the United States, the United Kingdom and Finland* (Helsinki: The Finnish Economic Association).

Lerner, E. 1956. "Inflation in the Confederacy 1861–65," in M. Friedman (ed.), *Studies in the Quantity Theory of Money* (Chicago: University of Chicago Press).

Lucas, R. E., Jr. 1972. "Expectations and the Neutrality of Money," *Journal of Economic Theory*, 4 (September), 103–124.

Macesich, G. 1970. "Supply and Demand for Money in Canada," in D. Meiselman (ed.), *Varieties of Monetary Experience* (Chicago: University of Chicago Press).

Marty, A. 1961. "Gurley and Shaw on Money in a Theory of Finance," *Journal of Political Economy*, 69 (February), 56–62.

Matthews, R. C. O. 1963. "Expenditure Plans and the Uncertainty Motive for Holding Money," *Journal of Political Economy*, 71 (June), 201–218.

Melitz, J. 1976. "Inflationary Expectations and the French Demand for Money 1959–70," *Manchester School*, 44 (March), 17–41.

Meltzer, A. H. 1963. "The Demand for Money: The Evidence from the Time Series," *Journal of Political Economy*, 71 (June), 219–246.

Meyer, P. A. and Neri, J. A. 1975. "A Keynes-Friedman Money Demand Function," *American Economic Review*, 65 (September), 610–623.

Michaelson, J. B. 1973. *The Term Structure of Interest Rates* (New York and London: Intext).

Niehans, J. and Schelbert-Syfrig, H. 1966. "Simultaneous Determination of Interest and Prices in Switzerland by a Two-Market Model for Money and Bonds," *Econometrica*, 34 (April), 408–413.

Orr, D. 1970. *Cash Management and the Demand for Money* (New York and London: Praeger).

Patinkin, D. 1965. *Money, Interest and Prices*, 2nd ed. (New York: Harper and Row).

Perlman, M. 1970. "International Differences in Liquid Assets Portfolios," in D. Meiselman (ed.), *Varieties of Monetary Experience* (Chicago: University of Chicago Press).

Pesek, B. P. and Saving, T. R. 1967. *Money, Wealth and Economic Theory* (New York: Macmillan).

Pifer, H. W. 1969. "A Nonlinear, Maximum Likelihood Estimate of the Liquidity Trap," *Econometrica*, 37 (April), 324–332.

Pigou, A. C. 1917. "The Value of Money," *Quarterly Journal of Economics*, 37 (November), 38–65.

Price, L. L. D. 1972. "The Demand for Money in the United Kingdom—A Further Investigation," *Bank of England Quarterly Bulletin*, 12 (March), 43–55.

Sargent, T. J. and Wallace, N. W. 1975. "Rational Expectations and the Theory of Economic Policy," Federal Reserve Bank of Minneapolis, *Studies in Monetary Economics*, 2.

Saving, T. 1971. "Transactions Cost and the Demand for Money," *American Economic Review*, 61 (June), 407–420.

Selden, Richard. 1956. "Monetary Velocity in the United States," in M. Friedman (ed.), *Studies in the Quantity Theory of Money* (Chicago: University of Chicago Press).

Shapiro, A. A. 1973. "Inflation, Lags, and the Demand for Money," *International Economic Review*, 14 (February), 81–96.

Smith, W. L. 1956. "A Graphical Exposition of the Complete Keynesian System," *Southern Economic Journal*, 23 (October), 115–125.

Spitzer, J. J. 1976. "The Demand for Money, the Liquidity Trap and Functional Forms," *International Economic Review*, 17 (February), 220–227.

Starleaf, D. R. and Reimer, R. 1967. "The Keynesian Demand Function for Money: Some Statistical Tests," *Journal of Finance*, 22 (March), 71–76.

Tanner, J. E. 1969. "Lags in the Effects of Monetary Policy: A Statistical Investigation," *American Finance Review*, 59 (December), 794–805.

Teigen, R. 1964. "Demand and Supply Functions for Money in the United States," *Econometrica*, 32, no. 4 (October), 477–509.

——. 1971. "The Demand for Money in Norway 1959–1969," *Statokonomisk Tidsskrift*, 3, 65–99.

Tobin, J. 1947. "Liquidity Preference and Monetary Policy," *Review of Economics and Statistics*, 29 (May), 124–131.

——. 1956. "The Interest Elasticity of Transactions Demand for Cash," *Review of Economics and Statistics*, 38 (August), 241–247.

——. 1958. "Liquidity Preference as Behavior towards Risk," *Review of Economic Studies*, 25 (February), 65–86.

Tucker, D. 1966. "Dynamic Income Adjustment to Money Supply Changes," *American Economic Review*, 56 (June), 433–449.

Vogel, R. C. 1974. "The Dynamics of Inflation in Latin America, 1950–1969," *American Economic Review*, 64 (March), 102–114.

Walters, A. A. 1965. "Professor Friedman on the Demand for Money," *Journal of Political Economy*, 73 (October), 545–551.

Whalen, E. L. 1966. "A Rationalisation of the Precautionary Demand for Cash," *Quarterly Journal of Economics*, 80 (May), 314–324.

Index